# JOHNATHAN IVEY

## The Man Behind The Monster

CHARLIE DYKSTRA

ISBN 978-1-64258-434-9 (paperback)
ISBN 978-1-64258-436-3 (hardcover)
ISBN 978-1-64258-435-6 (digital)

Copyright © 2018 by Charlie Dykstra

All rights reserved. No part of this publication may be reproduced, distributed, or transmitted in any form or by any means, including photocopying, recording, or other electronic or mechanical methods without the prior written permission of the publisher. For permission requests, solicit the publisher via the address below.

Christian Faith Publishing, Inc.
832 Park Avenue
Meadville, PA 16335
www.christianfaithpublishing.com

*Scripture taken from the New King James Version. Copyright © 1982 by Thomas Nelson, Inc. Used by permission. All rights reserved.*

Printed in the United States of America

First and foremost, to our LORD and SAVIOR JESUS CHRIST.

Also, to Johnathan Ivey himself for his inspirational example of how far we can push ourselves when we do it for love, and Savannah Ivey, the precious little girl who inspired a monster to become a loving Christian dad who would stop at nothing to take care of her!

Special thanks, to each person interviewed or otherwise recorded in this book. To my friends indeed at my times of need, Carla Fox Sanders for her photography and Michael Fox for his nonstop help and chauffeuring as we traveled! Also, to Dave Ramsey, for his book *The Total Money Makeover*, which helped me beat my financial burdens so I could pursue my goals debt free and without worry!

# Contents

| | | |
|---|---|---|
| Chapter 1 | Meeting the Monster and the Man | 7 |
| Chapter 2 | Where Did the Monster Come From? | 14 |
| Chapter 3 | Getting into Fighting | 19 |
| Chapter 4 | Making Ends Meet | 23 |
| Chapter 5 | The Hard Life of a Fighter | 29 |
| Chapter 6 | The Girl That Made It All Happen | 36 |
| Chapter 7 | The Monster's Classic Battles | 45 |
| Chapter 8 | The Bad Apple | 61 |
| Chapter 9 | Romancing the Monster | 70 |
| Chapter 10 | First Impressions | 77 |
| Chapter 11 | The Stress of Johnathan Ivey's First Show | 83 |
| Chapter 12 | The Monster's Return to the Cage | 89 |
| Chapter 13 | The Monster at the Crossroads | 94 |
| Chapter 14 | The Light at the End of the Tunnel of Stress | 98 |
| Chapter 15 | Road Trip to Kokomo | 102 |
| Chapter 16 | Meeting Ivey's Crowd | 112 |
| Chapter 17 | The Moment of Truth | 118 |
| Chapter 18 | Ivey's Second Show: The Other Moment of Truth | 125 |
| Chapter 19 | From Monster to Mentor | 129 |
| Chapter 20 | God Was Always There | 138 |
| Chapter 21 | Where Do We Go from Here? | 143 |

CHAPTER 1

# Meeting the Monster and the Man

> Therefore let us not judge one another anymore,
> but rather resolve this, not to put a stumbling
> block or cause to fall in our brother's way.
> —Romans 14:13 (NKJV)

No one could ever guess what the Leg Lock Monster is really like by his appearance. It would take a book about him to help people to understand who he is. So I am writing one. My task is to explain the single most complex, intriguing, and surprisingly honorable person I have ever known.

After years of bonding with the monster, he asked me to do his biography. Writing the life story of Johnathan Ivey is a complicated thing. The first thing that came to my mind was where even to begin? My first effort is to just break the ice on it all, and then I will tell from the very beginning how an underprivileged child became a legendary fighter and father in a category all his own.

As soon as Johnathan and I became friends, I noticed we were opposites. We both loved mixed martial arts (MMA), but that is where the similarities ended. I may have made almost all conservative decisions in life and kept my dreams restricted to hobbies. He, on the other hand, shunned all practicality and fulfilled his dreams with total determination at the expense of many beneficial things. Perhaps that is why we mix so well. I became a voice of reason in his reckless life, and he became an inspiration to chase dreams in my boring one. We talked about this many times.

I have often said, "Most people choose a path, Ivey built his own." He agrees with my statement. No one would find the life he created for himself practical, or even imaginable!

For me, it all started that night I first noticed the Leg Lock Monster. When I was cage side at an MMA show in Clarksville, Tennessee. Johnathan Ivey was a guest celebrity referee that night. A fighter I coached, Brandon Taylor, was fighting, and I was cornering for him.

When I looked at this ref, I saw lots of tattoos, big muscles, and no neck. He was a beast of a man, and at one point smiled, revealing a mouth full of gold teeth. My reaction was to say "That is the toughest-looking ref I have ever seen."

Brandon won his match with a quick technical knockout by taking his opponent down to the ground before unloading everything he had with punches. When Ivey tried to stop the fight, Brandon failed to yield. Brandon was so excited he fired off a flurry of punches just as Ivey called for the end of the contest. Being so focused on victory, Brandon did not even realize it was over.

The next thing I knew, Ivey threw Brandon off of his downed opponent—very literally threw him! My fighter, who was a big muscular man, came flying across the cage toward me and bounced off the side of the cage right in front of me before he landed! I remember yelling, "That ref just threw my cage fighter at me!" Then I laughed when I realized how funny that sounded. I liked Ivey already at that point. He reminded me slightly of Harry from the movie *Harry and the Hendersons*. A gentle monster who damaged everything around him, not realizing his strength. Talk about a first impression! You don't forget people who throw fighters at you.

Years later, as friends, we talked about that night and soon found the video online of him throwing Brandon Taylor all the way across the cage. Ivey, who had forgotten all about it, now said, "I shouldn't have thrown him like that." But even Brandon thought it was amusing and had no hard feelings. Ivey was acting in the safety of a downed fighter; he is just way better and more humorous at it than most refs.

Soon after that first meeting, I heard many things about the reputation of the Leg Lock Monster. He had set three world records and still holds two of them to this day. He was an MMA legend.

His name, the Leg Lock Monster, had been given to him from one of those world records. Leg locks are a very skilled art of manipulating any of the joints connected to the legs to cause either submission from pain or debilitating injury. Ivey had broken bones many times on his opponents when they failed to submit fast enough. The first record is he had defeated more fighters with leg locks than any professional cage fighter in history. *Tapout Magazine*, a national publication, wrote an article about Ivey entitled "The Leg Lock Monster," and the nickname stuck, replacing "Big John Ivey," as some called him at that time. No doubt those who fell prey to his leg locks understood the name "Leg Lock Monster" all too well!

The second world record he holds is even more impressive to me. He had fought more fights in a single year than any fighter in professional fighting history. During this time in 2003, he fought sick, injured, and often didn't know who he would be fighting. Sometimes he was not offered the match until the day of the fight. The number of matches for that one-year period was twenty-six, going beyond boldness and flirting with insanity!

Many would say there could be no good reason to risk your health and life in such a violent way, but they would be wrong. I would say the same until I knew the whole story, but Ivey had a great reason. As he explained, "I needed the money to take care of my baby girl." His motive is one of the key things that makes him such a warrior, but even more, an exceptional person and dad. His motivation was love, and he did this because it was the only way he knew how to provide for his new baby girl. Ivey is a single dad, but I will reveal those details in a later chapter where we can take the time to do them justice.

I also remember the night I met the man behind the monster more personally. My best friend, Michael K. Fox, and I were always at the local MMA shows for one reason or another. Frequently, we were both either ISKA officials or cornering our fighters, or sometimes just helping set up the cage.

One night, there was a show at a nightclub in Clarksville, Tennessee, that neither of us was involved in, so we just bought tickets and went. The advertisement failed to mention it was an outdoor show, located behind the club. It was a frigid, damp night in October, and we were freezing. We saw a T-shirt stand, so we decided to buy some and use the extra layer for warmth.

We both liked the same black Johnathan Ivey Leg Lock Monster shirt and bought the matching shirts. After putting them on, we returned to our seats. While sitting in the darkness waiting for the show to start, we heard a voice behind us say, "I like those shirts!" We turned to see a big guy in the dark who shook our hands and humbly thanked us for buying the shirts. I assumed he owned the stand that sold the shirts; it still seemed odd, him being so grateful.

When the show started, the guest celebrity referee was Johnathan Ivey. Fox looked at me and said that was the guy who thanked us for buying the shirts. I had not realized this due to the dark. He had gone out of his way to express his appreciation for our support. Later, as I got to know Ivey better, I would find out how sincerely moved he is by every individual supporter.

A few years passed, with us often bumping into each other. I had settled in as the primary timekeeper used in my area, Fox as a regular when anyone needed a judge, and Ivey was everyone's first choice as ref. So interactions at MMA shows became frequent.

Then he relocated for a short while to Huntingdon, Tennessee, near my area and wandered into the gym that Fox and I ran as a hobby. We got to be friends, and it was a great honor to have such a skilled professional fighting legend train in our amateur MMA gym. The fighters found him inspiring, and he gladly took time out to encourage them.

We never sparred full contact for safety reasons, but I often wrestled him. I always tried to keep him high on my body to avoid him reaching my legs due to his reputation. However, one time he put a leg lock on me; it was a classic kneebar. From that day forward, I had one goal only: do not ever let this monster's hands reach my legs! He could have crippled me anytime he wanted; he was going light, but light with him was bad enough!

# JOHNATHAN IVEY: THE MAN BEHIND THE MONSTER

I remember back to when I first saw Ivey. I had noticed how brutal he looked: gold teeth, muscles, and tattoos. After seeing him throw Brandon Taylor, who was kind of beastly himself, I had expected him to have a big attitude problem. But he was sincerely humble. His personality was in layers. Appearance well hid it, but he had some surprising fears and insecurities, along with a bit of a temper fueled by those insecurities. Hidden inside that was a sensitive and kindhearted Christian man. Ivey was no ordinary athlete; he was a great person, in a very intimidating exterior.

We continued to grow closer as friends. The real bonding process began while Ivey was preparing for a fight. After a few handshakes with our fighters and some conversation, we were honored to use our team to help him get ready for his next challenge in the cage. What he wanted is called shark tanking. We had done this often, one fighter spars back to back with every other fighter to build up his cardio. With no rest, they face new opponents who jump in fresh. However, his version was different: he spars with each person not just once, but switches out every 3 minutes for a whole hour!

There was six of us there that night, I think. There was a seventh, but he took one look at Ivey and refused to spar. I remember Brannon Philips, a kickboxer with a mohawk; Shelton Moon a larger judo competitor who had recently won a freestyle grappling grand championship, the coaches Fox and myself with a few others.

I thought Ivey was crazy; no one has an hour of fight in them! We were not on his level, of course, but an hour is a very long time. He went the whole sixty minutes without ever getting submitted, and the rest of us did plenty of tapping out to his submission holds.

Each of us faced him several times that night. He threw in a few of his classic showy moves to be funny, and the guys found him very entertaining. He would go all defense until the timer sounded the thirty-second warning, then he would begin trying to submit us, but take care not to hurt anyone. After training, we hung out at a local restaurant, and the young fighters were very inspired to interact socially with such a legend.

After years of growing as friends, we were messaging on Facebook one day, and he dropped a bomb on me. He said he was getting too old to fight anymore. He mentioned how punches that he used to eat were now rattling him. He was over forty now. Worst of all was that he was "a fighter and only a fighter." He had no other skills. He had nothing lined up for his future and no retirement or savings to fall back on for his older years.

He explained that he was going to try promoting but had no experience. Since Fox and I had some experience, we agreed to help. Our friendship started to grow much closer. I got to know the real man behind the monster. He became an open book to me as I had gained his trust.

I would have to say, Johnathan Ivey is a unique individual, with clashing qualities unlike any other person I have ever met. Ivey's curious supporters have many unanswered questions. I mentioned this and said he needed a biography; he asked me to do it myself. It was my turn to be humbled. I had done some ghostwriting for spoiled, lazy creative writing students and written several unfinished books and was about to attempt publishing my first one in the self-help category, but I was a rookie. Ivey didn't care; he wanted an author he could trust with his life story.

I would soon learn he deals only with people he is sure are trustworthy. His trust issues were one of the reasons he has limited his interactions with people and surrounds himself with a very select crowd.

There are way more qualified authors for this task, I thought, but none who know the monster as I do, so I accepted his offer. He explained to me that he had been talking about a biography for years, but he wanted something specific. He wanted his life story to lead people to find CHRIST like he had, and he wanted Bible verses matching the topic of each chapter. I had spent twenty years in the pulpit as a gospel preacher, so we were well matched for this effort.

We agreed to a tell-all story that would not candy-coat the negative things; the readers should know the real man behind the Leg Lock Monster. Ivey made many mistakes before his conversion. He made some mistakes after his conversion. He is learning and growing because that is what disciples do. My goal in the chapters to follow is to reveal to the readers this man that they would otherwise never really know.

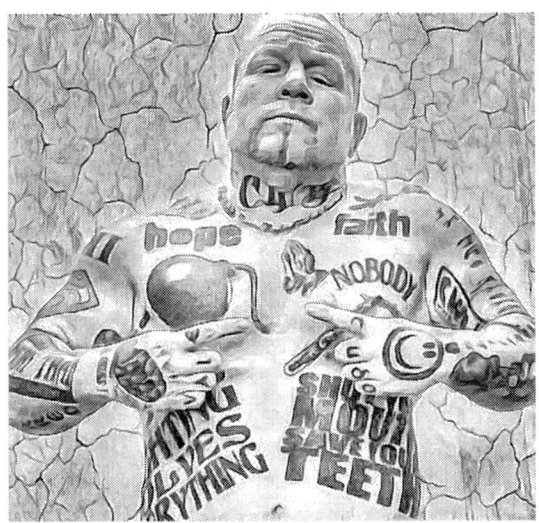

Johnathan Ivey, the Leg Lock Monster.

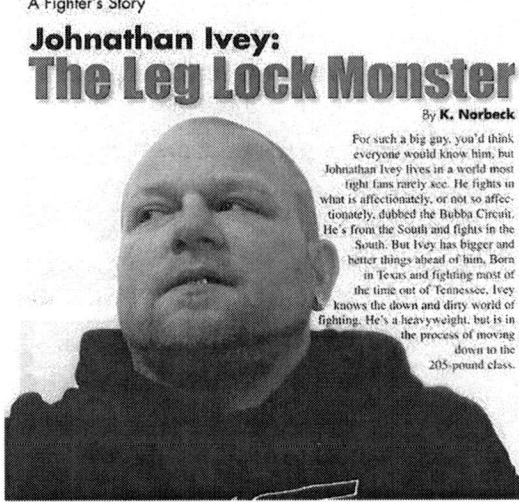

This article gave Ivey his nickname "the Leg Lock Monster."

CHAPTER 2

# Where Did the Monster Come From?

> Take heed that you do not despise one of these
> little ones, for I say to you that in heaven
> their angels always see the face of My Father who is in heaven.
> —Matthew 18:10 (NKJV)

Ivey's worst years for emotional struggles were sadly his youngest years, leading up to the seventh grade. Ivey has never met his father to this day, and his single mom struggled to provide. She continually held multiple minimum wage jobs at once in an attempt to provide for her young son.

Ivey lived those youthful years in a life tormented by pressures and conflicts. He faced bullying over his bad teeth, weight issues, unpopularity, insecurities, and poverty. His mother was forced to move often, and this added to the difficulty of making friends.

The absence of adult supervision and influence amounted to him raising himself, and the results were not a success story. He failed school a few times and cannot recall ever doing homework or studying in his entire youth.

In the fifth grade, a teacher noted Ivey's interest in the game of chess. It was an odd clash for a kid who did not study or do homework to be very interested in a highly intellectual game. It is not easy for me to picture a small "Leg Lock Monster" focused on a chess set. Perhaps this is because it is hard to imagine Ivey in the fifth grade, unless I envision him with tattoos and gold teeth. Once a person knows the modern version of Ivey, anything else is unthinkable.

This teacher would allow him to not participate in class to practice the game, then drive him to chess tournaments on the weekends. Though this seems odd, the teacher could have been trying to use the one motivation Ivey had to build a self-betterment attitude perhaps. The entire picture would strongly indicate Ivey's youth may have been a tragic loss of great potential.

After Ivey won the county-level tournaments, the teacher signed him up for the local chess club, which was mostly against senior citizens. At this point, my imagination stretches to the limits: my picture now contains a fifth-grade Leg Lock Monster defeating elderly competition in a chess game. This image is an amusing one.

The same teacher who allowed him to practice chess instead of participating in class, failed him for not letting him complete the class work. This scenario was quite a blow for a child, to be encouraged to do something, then later condemned for doing it. But it would be far from the last betrayal Ivey experienced in life. Ivey failed again in the sixth grade. He and his mother moved around often, and as a result, he could not keep up.

These years were spent primarily in various places around Florida, Mississippi, and Texas living in impoverished neighborhoods. With his single mom working for minimum wage wherever she could find jobs, Ivey faced dangerous daily survival. He was alone and vulnerable, often bullied. He would avoid trouble for self-preservation. Skipping school became a survival tactic at times, and once, after receiving death threats from a group of bullies, he decided to miss a month of school to avoid them. He and his mother relocated once again shortly after this truancy.

Ivey's life appeared to be a heartbreaking tragedy in which he was destined to be a sad statistic with a tragic ending. In my experience as a Christian youth counselor, I have seen too many of these stories end as grievously as you expect. However, one observation I have made is that in almost every case I have seen, the victim has a God-given out if they can find it and act on it. Some kids are smart and can use scholarships to escape their sad life; others seek apprenticeships to use their vocational skills, and some just join the military, which offers instant housing, pay, and job training. Ivey found his way out and is a prime example of what meaningful activities can do for misguided children. For all that was against him, Ivey discovered sports in the seventh grade and focused his rage on the determination to compete.

Ivey had moved again. This time from Beaumont, Texas, and he found himself in Coldspring, Texas, arriving on the day of seventh-grade-yearbook pictures for the track team. This day would be the turning point of his young life.

He was asked by the coach to try out and told to grab a jersey. There were only two left, and Ivey naturally reached for the biggest one, being a chubby kid. The most rugged athlete in the school, named Ervin Major, demanded the jersey from Ivey. The result was a fight. The sudden change in Ivey's life began to unfold from that moment. Ivey had unknowingly fought the most feared student in the school, making him a soberingly respected figure among the student body.

Next came the sports themselves. Football emerged as his passion. Soon he was a hero for his abilities on the football field. Ivey's tragic story relived through every move around multiple Southern states would now explode into a happy ending in Coldspring, Texas. For the first time in his life, he mattered. With his newfound purpose in life also came popularity. He heard the crowd cheering for him. Kids wanted to be his friend. He had found happiness.

Texas has the rule "No pass no play." Ivey found himself now getting good grades during football season, but still inferior during the offseason. The grades issue is not uncommon to struggling students who are good athletes. Schools do what they must to keep the athletics programs generating much-needed revenues. He began to realize sports made him who he was, and they were his purpose.

The school allowed Ivey to skip the eighth grade and passed him on to high school. Since Ivey had failed twice, the school said he was too old for junior high school, and the high school wanted him for football. Everything looked good, and Ivey had the life he had always wanted.

Then came a tragic blow. His mother broke the news to him, it was once again time to move. All that he had worked for and built up, his whole world, was about to end once more. Having gotten to be friends with Ervin Major, the kid he fought on his first day of school in Coldspring, together they found a solution. After some discussion, all parties agreed that Ivey would be taken in by Ervin's family and remain in Coldspring Texas. He finished out his time in high school as a white houseguest in a black family.

Ivey remained in that home until he was expelled his senior year. The school told him that if he ever returned to the school grounds, they would call the police. Ivey soon moved to Oregon with a friend on a whim. He left with sixty dollars to his name and no job arrangements. Staying only three months, Ivey realized his numerous bad decisions would destroy him if he remained.

As an out, he accepted a scholarship to play football for Bethel University in McKenzie, Tennessee. It seemed he was on his way in life, but he was still not well groomed for college. A struggle with conforming to college rules would prove his undoing.

His college experience ended when he was kicked off the team for fighting in a football scrimmage. Technically in the scrimmage, the agreement is no sacking the quarterback; however, Ivey felt that if he worked hard enough to bust through the line, he should get the credit for sacking the quarterback. The tackle was more of a suplex, slamming the quarterback excessively hard on his back, and it brought a violent response from the offensive line who came to the rescue. Ivey ended up fighting the entire offensive line, and the results of that were the end of his scholarship.

Ivey returned home to Texas and his rough crowd, his friends were always in trouble, and he knew his life would not go well if he stayed. After some soul-searching, he called the coach and begged for another chance. The coach agreed, and Ivey returned to Bethel the following football season.

The second chance lasted about two weeks before he was kicked out for fighting once again. The fight this time was with the defensive line over a smart remark made to him during cone drills. One could say that Ivey doesn't start fights, but he is near incapable of walking away from one.

The solution came when Ivey transferred to Clarksville, Tennessee, to play football for Austin Peay State University. However, that university is under NCAA rules, which state that he must take a full year of classes before being eligible to play. It was during this year that he got introduced to mixed martial arts. His youth ended, and his legendary career was about to begin.

A rare photo of the "Leg Lock Monster" at age 3.

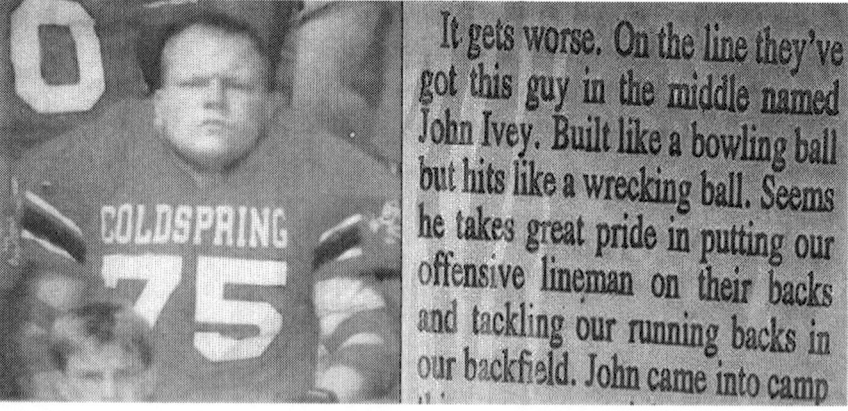

A newspaper clipping from Johnathan Ivey's high school football days.

CHAPTER 3

# Getting into Fighting

Whatever your hand finds to do, do it with your might.
—Ecclesiastes 9:10 (NKJV)

During Ivey's first year in Clarksville, Tennessee, he was powerlifting at a local gym. He became distinguished at the gym by the other weightlifters and was nicknamed Tank after UFC fighter Tank Abbott. He was unfamiliar with mixed martial arts at the time, and Tank Abbott was the very first bad boy of the sport. What Ivey did not know at that time was that Abbott would soon be his inspiration to be an MMA fighter and his all-time favorite fighter.

Weightlifting resulted in Ivey breaking an American Powerlifting Association (APA) junior world record when he bench-pressed 610 pounds. He was an inspiration among the lifters there. I interviewed Sam Taylor, a weightlifter friend of Ivey's for the past twenty years, who met him at that gym. Sam said with Ivey coaching him, he gained one hundred pounds on his bench pressing maximum. When Ivey won a bench pressing contest on a Wednesday night, it earned him the attention of Tommy Graham, a heavyweight cage fighting champion from the Hook & Shoot organization.

Graham walked him two doors down from the contest to a small fight gym and showed him just two moves for about twenty minutes, a key lock and a guillotine choke hold. The following Friday, Graham took him to see a four-man Hook & Shoot tournament. This MMA event would be Ivey's introduction to the sport of MMA, which at that time was still called no holds barred (NHB), having far fewer rules and being bare-knuckle.

As fate would have it, one of the four fighters did not show up. This would be Ivey's invitation to the sport of professional fighting. Ivey got asked to fill the opening, which he agreed to do. Armed with only two moves in his arsenal and an amateur record of no wins or losses, Ivey won his debut fight in forty-two seconds by a guillotine choke hold. He was severely disadvantaged by knowing only two moves, but all he needed was one of those two for the win. The following night, he added a second pro win, beating Chad Bartlett in twelve seconds when Bartlett tapped out due to strikes. This second win came just three days after meeting Tommy Graham at that contest.

Ivey had now learned that people got paid to fight, and he needed money. Since he often found himself in fights, he concluded that fighting for free is dumb when you can get paid. This decision would put the fork in his path from football to MMA. A lifestyle he never veered from to this day. The thug teenager who played football was evolving into the Leg Lock Monster, all as a result of fate and chance meetings.

During his Hook & Shoot fights, some of the staff labeled Ivey "the Tank Abbott of Hook & Shoot." He gained fame fast as he would go on to fight on eleven Hook & Shoot cards. Nine matches were MMA, and two were tag team grappling. In a bit of a twist to the sport, he did one of those two matchups, dressed as horror movie slasher Michael Myers. Though that may sound more like pro wrestling, this was real; he just enjoyed entertaining the crowd with his love for horror. This horror theme would evolve with Ivey as he incorporated it into his entertaining ring entrances.

With the Hook & Shoot experience, as well as what was gained fighting for other promotions, Ivey was soon well established as a force in the sport of MMA. However, he had climbed faster than his lack of training had prepared him. With the total absence of an amateur foundation, he soon found himself thrown in with established cage fighting veterans much better trained than himself. The sport has always had brawlers with less training who attempted to slug their way to wins with power and striking intensity over technique, Ivey was ironically the grappling version of this. Ivey combined the power and intense brawling, but with his system of submission grappling to finish opponents quickly before their experience and training could defeat him. This unique combo put Ivey in the category all his own but still had him disadvantaged against the best-trained greats of MMA that he soon encountered.

When UFC veteran Jeremy Horn became the champion of Hook & Shoot, Ivey fought as a considerable underdog against Horn. Ivey was still relatively new and only roughly trained. Horn had earlier that year choked UFC fighter Chuck Liddell unconscious, a reminder to Ivey that he was in with the top fighters in MMA now. Ivey was terrified, but it was not like him to turn down a big fight. He was a self-proclaimed basket case. He ended up aggravating a former bench pressing injury and lost the fight by default.

The emotional weakness of Ivey emerged as his Achilles' heel in the sport. In fact, half of his fights in his early career, he would fight drunk to calm his nerves. Ivey rolled with the punches and gained experience the hard way. He grew with the sport, as neither it nor he was well established at this point.

The first decade or two of MMA were unpredictable years for the struggling sport. Ivey often traveled far to newer promotions that had unchallenging competition. He would win with ease, but the promoter would lose money on the event and vanish. Many of Ivey's wins went unrecorded as a result, which was very discouraging. In truth, Ivey has fought more than two hundred fights (counting sanctioned and unsanctioned), and most all of those unrecorded fights were the easy wins in smaller promotions.

Despite all these discouragements, Ivey persevered year after year, accepting fights against all in his path. He never allowed himself to get hung up on his record but focused on the payday to earn a living for him and his daughter. He continued to take short-notice matchups with little or no preparation, year after year. Perhaps this was a dangerous game plan, but it was a promoter's dream come true. Ivey was the fighter who would save the card, filling in at the last minute, and his number was on the promoters' speed dial.

## CHARLIE DYKSTRA

The Leg Lock Monster after winning his first MMA title—the Extreme Combat International (ECI) Heavyweight Championship.

CHAPTER 4

# Making Ends Meet

*And my God shall supply all your need according
to His riches in glory by Christ Jesus.*
—Philippians 4:19 (NKJV)

There is a great misconception that cage fighters get paid massive amounts of money. When I mentioned to one of the amateur MMA guys that Johnathan Ivey was now promoting fights, he replied, "It's easy for him, he is rich." But the truth is, cage fighting is still a new, growing sport. The big paydays are few and far between. In fact, some world champions worked a full-time day job right up until winning the title.

Johnathan averages less than five thousand dollars per fight, and that is after many years of gaining fame. Needless to say, as a single parent, he must supplement his income. He is not the kind of person who delivers pizza in the evenings to pay off his mortgage like I did. To quote him, "Fighting is all I know." Like every other angle of his life, his supplemental incomes have been daring and colorful.

The closest thing to a regular job with a shift he has had so far would be a rather brief career as a not-well-paid bouncer. The job lasted two weeks. It ended when he choked a customer unconscious for calling him Butterbean. As he sincerely explained to me, he had no choice, because the man called him that in front of girls. (We both laughed.) We had reached a point in our relationship where I could tease him, and I sarcastically replied, "Of course, this man must die."

He was valuable as a bouncer. The owners of the nightclub said they would allow him to stay if he would promise it would never happen again. He said he could not do that, and his career as a bouncer ended.

Another source of income, but not high-paying supplemental income, was playing semi-pro football. Being well experienced in both high school and college football, plus being beastly athletic, this worked out well for him. Ivey negotiated for one hundred dollars per game and all new equipment, "the good stuff." By his admission, he is a big diva. He likes things of quality. He enjoyed football, but needless to say, it was not a financial solution or a career.

A steady flow of small income has been from T-shirt sales. He has sold over ten thousand shirts. His trademark slogan on the back of every shirt is "Shut Your Mouth, Save Your Teeth." These shirts have been popular with his MMA supporters for fifteen years.

Interestingly, some people seek out the shirts just because they like the slogan. They sometimes are purchased by non-MMA fans. One gas station attendant recently asked Fox to get her one when she saw his. Fox did get her one from Ivey, and he was laughing about how she ran and put it on immediately. She explained that in her job, she has a lot of patrons who are difficult to deal with, and she wanted the shirt to forewarn them she was not putting up with them.

As I mentioned in the opening chapter, Ivey was a referee, and a great one. I spoke with former World Kickboxing champion Anthony Maness, now working for the ISKA who sanctions MMA events in Tennessee, concerning Ivey as a referee. Maness spoke of Ivey as being on a whole new level as a ref. He mentioned that they have never had an MMA death in the state of Tennessee, but if it were not for Ivey, they would have.

Maness explained the details of the incident of which he spoke. One of the hardest-hitting amateur MMA fighters at the time was Matt Brown. Brown got matched in Crossville against another of the hardest hitters. The two fighters both chose to go toe to toe and punch it out. Matt knocked out his opponent, but it was one of those rare knockouts where the victim is unconscious but still standing. Ivey sensed what was happening and jumped in to stop the fight. Many referees with less experience would not have stopped a fight in which the contestant was still standing and active. I thought that was the end of the story. It was not.

Later that night the fighter who lost became unresponsive. He had to be life-flighted. The hospital found multiple bleeds on his brain. He lived, and would not have if Ivey didn't stop the action when he did. Anthony Maness was adamant about the fact Ivey saved the man's life. As he pointed out, that kind of ability as a ref is not something you can teach—it must be learned by experience.

Being a referee was perfect for him, but there is not a fight card every night of the week. Ivey makes a few hundred a night, but of course, travel expenses significantly reduce profit margins. This source of income became one of many that trickled survival money into his pocket but did not gain him financial security.

He was making a few hundred per week to teach all the MMA classes at several gyms in Clarksville for a long while. The money helped with a few bills, where his fight income fell short. He was good at it and well admired by fighters. But in time, he chose to move on to try new things.

The headaches of running a gym have always discouraged him from having one of his own. He has the notoriety to succeed at this, but not the desire. The primary concern is collecting dues. Ivey has a tender heart and has been an underprivileged kid himself; it is hard for him to confront and pressure people who lack the means. In the fight business, few patrons are wealthy. Collecting membership dues is almost always a struggle. Having run a fight gym myself, I agree with him on this. We would often have a dozen fighters offering to clean up or otherwise earn their keep, but not enough paying customers to balance the books. Ivey is more the one-night-wonder type, show up, show out, get paid, and go home.

The big, quick money was leg lock seminars. He would make several hundred in a single night. When the opportunities were there, he did a one night's crash course in the skills that made him famous, the art of manipulating leg joints.

Many seminars are more hype than instruction, but not Ivey's. He is the real master of what he does and has fighters' broken bones proving it. Ivey hates to speak in front of crowds; he will break the ice and then get down to business. For a fee, a gym can bring a legend in and enlighten their fighters in the art of joint manipulation, with no hype.

His unique fighting style of fast-paced submission grappling has caught a lot of interest in the Clarksville area. The highly successful Harris Holt Martial Arts Gym there often brings Ivey in for seminars. Lance Boyd, the MMA coach there, is one of Ivey's old friends and teaches Ivey's fighting system.

The ranking process does give Ivey a small bit of income, similar to traditional martial arts. Where there is a fee to test for rank. Ivey leaves this whole process to Lance, who has perfected the art of balancing uniformed martial arts and MMA in the same building.

Without a doubt, the most unexpected source of money Ivey has had is backyard brawling challenges. I say unexpected, because looking at him, I cannot imagine that someone sees this man and wants to call him out for a fight, but it has happened many times. It is not uncommon for brawlers to convince themselves they can beat real athletes. Ivey did not make this about ego but, rather, about income. He would ask them to put their money where their mouth was, and he would match any bet they placed on themselves.

As a promoter, I had met many who asked me to put them in the cage so they could test their brawling skills against a mixed martial artist. They were often handy for filling out a card, but all lost, and lost badly. But you can do that with amateurs, not pros. Backyard brawling is unsanctioned, comparable to barroom brawling.

Ivey has encountered many brawlers who were not impressed by him and quick to tell him. Ivey added a little income to his budget from these challenges. He accepted all challengers so long as they were willing to place a bet on themselves, and he never lost.

Ironically, the first night I met with Ivey for an interview, one of these brawlers happened into the same restaurant and greeted him with a handshake. Ivey had not only taken his money, but he earned the brawler's respect and admiration. He was genuinely pleased to get to see Ivey. The man was sitting reasonably far away; he could have gone unnoticed, but he chose to leave his party of eight and go out of his way to speak with Ivey. Ivey has that effect on people who get to know him, even those who become acquainted with him the hard way.

# JOHNATHAN IVEY: THE MAN BEHIND THE MONSTER

Most brawl challenges have been simple—a few hundred dollars' bet on a quick fight. Similar for Ivey to sparring in the gym, only this way, he makes money sparring. But one time the challenge became bigger. Jason DeFord, better known as the rapper Jelly Roll is a personal friend of Ivey's. Somehow a brawl challenge was discussed between Jason and another party that had some real money to throw around. The result was a wager of ten thousand dollars on a fight between Ivey and a fighter representing the other man.

Ivey was very excited for this, but when the other fighter learned who he was to brawl, he declined. Ivey missed that big payday; brawling was just another trickle of income that had allowed this loving single dad to take good care of his little girl year after year.

Some would say perhaps the saddest way Ivey made money was selling the trophies and championship belts that he had won. It was not disturbing to him; he has no real use for such trinkets, it is not his style. The sales of these items helped pay bills, and that was what mattered to him. Most were not bought by collectors as memorabilia as you might expect, but by gym owners and coaches who would mislead customers into believing they had won those championships to build a name for themselves. Ivey did not miss these tokens at all and had no regrets; he laughs about it and the motive of those who purchased them.

The most amusing small income Ivey ever made, at least in my opinion, is from foot racing. Sam Taylor, Ivey's longtime friend who owned a concrete company in Clarksville talked about this when I interviewed him. He told me about their adventures setting up the foot races for Ivey against his concrete construction workers. At his peak weight, Ivey tipped the scales at over three hundred pounds. By wearing baggy clothing, he appeared to be out of shape, overweight and looked like he would be quite slow. This appearance would give a false confidence to slender young men who would bet money they could beat Ivey in a race. Ivey was always heavy, but a colossal athlete; he never lost at foot racing, nor failed to collect the cash he had won.

None of these incomes were careers. None had long-term or steady, or even dependable, income. Ivey has made a life of them anyway. Some people live paycheck to paycheck. He lives opportunity to opportunity, and all of them involve fighting one way or another.

Perhaps he is reckless, but he is doing what every athlete dreams of doing, surviving off his athletic abilities. He has succeeded, and he is here for his daughter. No one can deny either. He provides for his family, and they have not done without anything they need. When we take an honest look at the list of incomes, we see nothing huge except the heart of the man that makes them.

Johnathan Ivey seconds after knocking out his opponent in one of his many challenge brawls.

The big paydays are few and far between.

## CHAPTER 5

# The Hard Life of a Fighter

> My brethren, count it all joy when you fall into various trials, knowing that the testing of your faith produces patience.
> —James 1:2–3 (NKJV)

Money is far from the only struggle for a fighter. The list of battles is very long indeed. In this chapter, I will attempt to hit the highlights of the brutal life Ivey accepted to provide for his daughter. To do justice to this topic, however, would require a separate book.

Often people view facts from too shallow a perspective. We hear of a pro fighter getting a world title shot, a big pay-per-view event, or some other infrequent opportunity; then we may think of that every time any fighter fights. However, that was one highlight out of a long career with decades of training, sacrifice, travel, and strained relationships. The highest paydays and short-lived glory divided by the years of sacrifices soon make even those rare peaks of a fighting career look unrewarding. Most fighters never reach that level. It is a hard road; all who choose it are to face intimidating odds.

Ivey was a street fighter when he first heard of mixed martial arts. He did not even have any basic martial arts training, like karate or judo. To jump straight into the pros is suicidal, but that was what Ivey chose to do, and the results were an even rougher road than most fighters experience. Ivey could not imagine fighting for free once he learned he could get paid. He was reckless, yes, but that is in a word how you could describe his whole life and career.

After jumping into the pros, his adventure began, and it was a painful one. During Ivey's career, he has never had health insurance. He has faced many injuries, and his theory has always been that he would just lie in bed until he healed. His self-designed health plan is one example of his typical life decisions, but he has made it, and no one can deny that.

His heal-in-bed theory may sound like a joke, but once, he spent a month in bed after a significant back injury in a Wisconsin matchup. He had to be driven back to Tennessee lying flat on the floor of a van. He lay in bed for a full thirty days to heal, finally able to get around with just one day before leaving for a match with Jimmy Ambriz for the King of the Cage Super Heavy Weight Championship in Albuquerque, New Mexico, on a national television pay-per-view.

Ivey explained the fight was a good paycheck, he just plain needed the money, so he got out of bed and went. After his flight arrived, he was given a casino food voucher and ate a meal that gave him massive food poisoning. When he returned to his room at the casino, he experienced such projectile vomiting and was unable to make it to the bathroom. The room required such extensive cleanup he was unable to sleep there that night.

This title fight was not one of his big wins, of course. The combination of illness and injury left him little chance, resulting in a first-round loss. Most any fighter would have pulled out of the match, but not Ivey. It is just not his way to pull out of a scheduled fight.

Though he has done well avoiding permanent damage, Ivey suffered one notable injury from which he has never fully recovered. In a match against the big-named fighter, Scott Barrett, Ivey sustained a broken orbital bone. His eye has never set right in the socket since.

I happened to be in the crowd the night that happened. We were not yet close friends, but Fox and I admired him enough to travel a few hours to support him. Ivey was doing impressively, then suddenly it was apparent something was wrong. He could no longer defend himself, the swelling had closed his eye completely, and he could no longer see punches coming to protect himself. The ref ended the fight, calling it for a technical knockout.

## JOHNATHAN IVEY: THE MAN BEHIND THE MONSTER

There have been other reasonably significant injuries, most of which Ivey ignored since he is uninsured. Those have all healed up over time. He has been blessed to fight for nineteen years and over two hundred fights in actual count, always recovering without the often-needed medical treatment.

The injuries are far from the only bad experience he has had in his career. Ivey agreed to travel to Nuevo Laredo, Mexico, to face Ben Brown. Ivey had been stiffed out of his pay one time before and was forced to take a loss on even his travel. Since then, Ivey insists on cash up front unless the promoter is a trusted friend.

He had heard rumors about the promotion and feared he would not get paid after the fights. He insisted they pay him in cash before he would leave his room to go to the show. The promotion had agreed to this, but did not come with the payment.

Ivey received a call with a promise of payment after the show; he refused to leave the room. Not long before the show was about to start, he got yet another call asking him to please come. Ivey again refused. The promoter who realized Ivey was not coming out without being paid rushed to his room and paid him the cash, in vast quantities of one- and five-dollar bills! The thrown-together roll of money and the stalling tactics strongly indicated the promoter had not prepared to pay him at all.

Ivey then rushed to the show to fight Ben Brown. Being considered the Bad Guy by the crowd, Ivey had full cans of beer thrown at him on his way to the cage. The night was not all bad, however. Despite the stress and turmoil, Ivey defeated Ben Brown by a kneebar in the first round.

Anytime you do anything enough times, bad things happen. It is just a fact of life. Race car drivers have blowouts, politicians slip up and say something damaging, doctors misdiagnose patients, and waitresses spill food. The Bible says, "Time and chance happen to them all" (Eccles. 9:11). MMA fighters are no exception to this rule.

Ivey has had several dozen professional fights and bad luck in some of them. Well-known UFC fighter Ben Rothwell was scheduled to fight Johnathan Ivey to decide the USMMA Heavyweight

Championship, in Boston, Massachusetts. Defeating Rothwell would catapult Ivey's career.

This match contained perhaps the worst luck of Ivey's career. In the first thirty seconds, Ivey cut himself severely on Rothwell's knee sleeve going for a takedown. The cut was above the eye. The referee paused the action for the medical staff to check Ivey's eye. They agreed to let it continue, and the match restarted.

Ivey took Rothwell down with a rolling kneebar attempt and came close to locking the hold on Rothwell. Seconds later, the referee stopped the fight due to the bleeding from the cut. Even Rothwell was surprised by the stoppage, landing a hard punch to Ivey after it was over. The referee exploded in a verbal rebuke at Rothwell, threatening to disqualify him. Rothwell stressed he had no idea it was over when he threw the last punch.

Rothwell immediately started apologizing for the late hit, and he looked sincere. Neither he nor Ivey wanted this to end the way it did. Bad luck happens, and way too often in the sport of MMA. The crowd booed loudly at the stoppage and chanted profanity in protest at the announcement of the results.

Both men showed their sportsmanship afterward, hugging each other in an act of exchanging mutual respect. Rothwell did little celebrating, barely holding up his new championship belt for a split second, then lowering it with a look of regret on his face. He shrugged his shoulders at the booing crowd and frowned as if to ask, what could he do about the way it went?

I watched the video online many times, trying to figure out how a knee sleeve caused such a cut, but never saw an explanation. One man gained a championship by happenstance that hurt his popularity, and the other lost the bout by the same misfortune. Both men went home without the feeling of victory that night. Such is the life of an MMA fighter.

*****

When Ivey was asked to fight UFC Hall of Fame fighter Dan Severn, it seemed he was finally on his way. Severn was an icon in mixed martial arts. He had been the top man in the early UFC and one of the best-known UFC fighters ever. Ivey felt positive about his career for the first time traveling to the event. His mind dwelt on the idea that he had finally gotten to where he worked so hard to be. After arriving at the airport, he was taken to the motel in the same SUV as Severn. Ivey sat directly behind Severn, noting the enormous sized head of Severn that looked intimidating.

Facing Dan Severn stands out in Ivey's mind for more reasons than fighting a UFC legend. This event was when he got a taste of the lifestyle of even the top competitors in the MMA business; it was not the five-star treatment he expected. When they arrived, he received a room at a sleazy motel, with a warm greeting from a used condom lying on the floor! This memory was Ivey's introduction to the luxurious life of MMA superstardom.

The harsh fighter's lifestyle is trading every practical thing you have in your life for a short, volatile career. You receive no benefits like health insurance, life insurance, retirement, paid vacation, or other negotiable perks that so many occupations have. Ivey has felt the effects of that loss many times.

The fighter's life is hard from every angle, including family, which Ivey craves. So far he has never found the right woman to fit into his fighter's lifestyle. Ivey wants very much to settle down, but as always, his daughter comes first, and he will not consider anyone who will not make a good mother for his child.

One sad fact is that when he arrived on the scene, the sport was new, and it was much easier to get the spotlight. With all due respect to the early classic fighters in MMA, many were ordinary people. These contestants had regular jobs and trained in their spare time. Many were straight stylists, using such approaches as karate, boxing, or kickboxing, which had almost no chance once the fight went to the ground. Ivey was one of the few full-time MMA fighters. These one-dimensional styles could not have likely competed with Ivey, but he did not get his opportunity.

He had trained with or fought many of those chosen for the UFC. I cannot name a single fighter that has squared off against more UFC veterans than Ivey has. Not even the UFC competitors themselves seemed to have faced as many. Ivey had some impressive wins over some and went the distance with several of the very best, including UFC Hall of Fame fighters Ken Shamrock and Dan Severn, as well as former UFC heavyweight champion Ricco Rodriguez. Shamrock and Severn are two of the all-time best-known UFC fighters, but after Ivey went the distance with both, he received no consideration from the UFC.

Some Ivey supporters have worn his shirts to the UFC events to protest this, but still, no offer ever came. He is now past the age of forty, and though the UFC has had fighters that old before, it is unlikely he will ever receive the offer. It was just not meant to be, apparently.

Perhaps the saddest part of never being allowed to fight in the UFC is the fight that never happened with Tank Abbott. Abbott was the original bad boy of mixed martial arts. Abbott had little ground-fighting ability, but had unbelievable punching power. Having knocked down former UFC champ Don Frye with just a jab and holding some of the most devastating knockouts in the sport. Ivey's inspiration was Tank Abbott; Ivey was the grappling version of Tank. Many fighters pointed this fact out to Ivey. Ivey even had Tank's face tattooed on his leg. He dreamt of the day he would fight his hero in the UFC, but it never happened. The dream fight that never happened is one of his saddest regrets of his career.

The rap artist Jelly Roll is a close friend of Ivey's and has a song called "Never Give Up." Ivey is in one version of the music videos, and the song seems to have been written about him and his struggles to support his daughter by fighting. As a rule, I hate rap music, but this has become one of my favorite songs. The song is both inspirational and meaningful, once I look past my many complaints about rap music. This one song raised the standard of rap for me.

# JOHNATHAN IVEY: THE MAN BEHIND THE MONSTER

Johnathan Ivey moments before the start of a fight in Atlanta, Georgia.

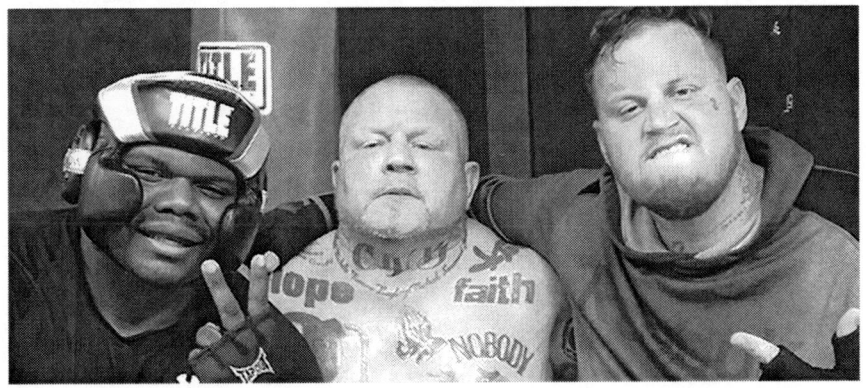

MMA fighter Robert "R-Dub" Williams, Johnathan Ivey, and rap artist Jelly Roll are all good friends that train together.

## CHAPTER 6

# The Girl That Made It All Happen

> But if anyone does not provide for his own, and
> especially for those of his household,
> he has denied the faith and is worse than a unbeliever.
> —1 Timothy 5:8 (NKJV)

Her name is Savannah Ivey. She is the girl who made it all happen. In many ways, this story is about her.

Ivey is a single father to a little girl as near perfect as children come. She was his motivation to go from just a fighter to a warrior who would fight twenty-six professional fights in a single year to provide for her. The record was unprecedented. No one had ever done it before, and most likely, no one will ever try again. The effects on a person's health, the insufficient healing time from injury between fights, and the impossibility of preparing for a particular opponent on short notice makes this record insane, almost suicidal. But Ivey did what he had to do to raise his child, and he did it amazingly well, breaking a second world record for the most leg lock wins in the process.

I have often watched nature films and seen bears, lions, or gorillas defend their young. I cannot help but think of this with Ivey. (Incidentally, he casually mentioned his favorite animal is the gorilla.) He needed to provide for his daughter, but one thing stood in his way, an opponent. As a result, he became the monster he had to be. Like with any beast, it was not an option; it just had to be, and so it was.

## JOHNATHAN IVEY: THE MAN BEHIND THE MONSTER

There were times he was in the audience and came to find out someone did not show up to fight, so he fought. He would cut a deal, borrow gear, and fight. There could be no doubt that Ivey's win/loss record would be way better if he did what other fighters do. Many take only fights they are confident they can win. They only target opponents whose weaknesses they can exploit and who cannot defend against their strengths. They study videos to know every detail about their rivals. They fight a few fights a year. If Ivey did that, he could not provide as well. Ivey would have a legendary win/loss record, but to provide for Savannah, he just fought everything in his path and accepted the abundance of disadvantages that come with that approach to fighting. There are many far worse fighters with far better records, but they will never be the warrior he is.

One of my favorite interviews in working with Ivey's biography, and a future documentary, is Savannah Ivey. She was thirteen at the time. I was anxious to meet the girl who made it all happen. My imagination ran wild trying to guess what Ivey's child would be like. The image of Ivey provokes creative thoughts of what a young Ivey offspring could be. All my guessing was wrong. The experience was a great honor, and I was impressed.

I was expecting a child full of insecurities and problems for obvious reasons. She was a girl raised by a single man, which is never an ideal situation. In her world, the next decent paycheck would be the next time her dad got in a steel cage and fought for his life, which carries a double feel of jeopardy—both injury and financial insecurity. Being interracial is much more accepted by the public these days, but she has faced a few verbal attacks at a young age for having a white father and a black mother, once being called Half Breed by some black adults. On top of this and other factors in her life, her dad is a fighter, not quite Dr. Phil. But Savannah was quite secure, well-balanced, intelligent, and lovable.

When the interview with Savannah happened, Ivey thought it best if he waited in the car so she could relax and feel no pressure with his presence when she and I met, since we would be talking about him. After we all had eaten a meal together to break the ice, I met with her at Dunkin Donuts, and was surprised any child could have such a combination of humility and yet open straightforward communication skills and complete trust in her father as a provider and dad. I could see no insecurities at all. She is very proud of Ivey and comfortably secure in her household.

I had first talked to Ivey about his relationship with Savannah, then Savannah about her relationship with Ivey. This way, I could build a solid perspective of their household from both points of view.

Ivey is protective of her. That is an understatement! He goes to every school orientation that parents are allowed. He makes it a point to dress in a wifebeater tank top and make eye contact with every boy who looks like a player or a troublemaker. He does not allow boyfriends, and she says she understands why and agrees it is stupid for girls her age to be in romantic relationships. I have often worked with youth groups, and after knowing dozens of parent/child relationships, I have never seen Ivey and Savannah's equals.

The nearest thing she has to a complaint is about not having a cell phone as all kids do. Ivey feels that is when the trouble will begin, when boys can go around him to influence her. He promised her a cell phone at age fifteen. She is looking forward to it; Ivey is not. She agrees he is right to be protective about this, but still wants one when the time comes. When my interview with her ended, later on, the phone topic had slipped my mind. I said, "Okay, text your dad and tell him he can come in now." She only looked at me and smiled, I suppose wondering if I was joking or not. I said, "Oh yeah, no phone, sorry." We both laughed about this.

I asked her, if she could change just one thing about her dad, what would she change? I was sure the answer would be the phone rule, but she said, "I wish he had a safer job and fewer tattoos." She has been to a few of his fights and gets too "worked up." Since she mentioned tattoos, I asked her if he has any tattoos she likes. She said without a pause, "My name." Ivey put "Savannah" around his neck, and she is very honored by this. He also has her picture on his left side, which she pointed out to him. "You put me in your armpit." In Ivey's defense, he did not have too many available spaces from which to choose!

Ivey had brought a video that night of her training. She was punching mitts, throwing the type of punches he called out. Savannah is adorable, thin, and feminine, but the punches were landing with a loud snapping sound. She could hit very hard. I asked her, with her dad being a ground fighter who loves leg locks, but her being so good at stand-up striking, which one did she like better? Savannah said with an innocent smile, "I am better at stand-up, but I like grappling better because I don't like getting punched in the face."

I agree with her. That is why I too was a grappler!

When asked about having only a father in her home, she said he is the mom and the dad. She has met her mother and liked her, holding no grudges over her absence. Savannah shows her positive attitude and kind heart since Ivey pointed out many times that she had gotten her hopes up about hearing from her mom and being disappointed. Savannah feels that Ivey has done a great job playing both parental roles, and she feels blessed. She describes both her parents in a positive light, but says she is much more like her dad than her mom.

When asked directly about her father's fighting career, she says she does approve, but with some concerns. Mostly Savannah worries, of course, for Ivey's safety. She said sincerely, "He says getting beat up don't hurt, but I know it does."

When I asked if her friends ever have anything to say about Ivey, she said: "They think it is cool that he is a pro fighter and never say anything bad about him, but they might be afraid to."

Being thrown by a teenager who is so upbeat about a parent, I decided to challenge Savannah a little, so I asked her, are there any issues she and her dad strongly disagree over?

Her response was quick and confident. "Roller coasters and horror movies."

It was not at all what I expected to hear. She then said, "He says they are not scary, but they are."

Ivey mentioned the same; he said he made a mistake exposing her to both too young. She was not ready for either and formed a firm opinion on them at an early age.

Since she brought up the topic of horror movies, I asked her if she watched *Fearsville II*, in which her dad had a guest starring role playing himself. They had watched it together, so I asked if it was hard watching him die in the film. She said, "Yes, but he was right there beside me when I saw him die, so that made it easier." She was also in the movie as an extra portraying a trick-or-treater.

Since we were on the topic of movies, I asked what role she would like to see Ivey play in the next film he does. Savannah said with a glowing expression, "A comedy character, like Jack Black or Adam Sandler, but I could more see him playing the killer in a horror movie."

When I asked Ivey what his dream role would be, he said he wanted to play Deathrattle, who is the demon-possessed mob hit man in a horror book I have written but not yet published. I agreed he is perfect for the part. I have never met a parent and a child who know each other as well as they do!

I asked Savannah, what does she want for Ivey's future? Her reply was simple: retire before he gets injured, and just promote fight cards and do movies. She is considering being a fighter and hopes her dad will be able to travel to the fights with her if she does. She sees other options for herself since she loves animals, especially Tiger, her dog. She might be a vet. I could not help but notice how she automatically tied her dad's future to her own. They are undeniably close.

When we discussed the biography, she had the opportunity to say what she wants to see put in it. She said, "I want this book to say everything about him." Ivey wants the same—a tell-all book with the good and the bad. He had been quoted online when announcing the biography, "Some of you may like me better, some of you may not like me as much." These two even think alike.

In other areas of her young life, Savannah says she likes school and gets mostly A's, but occasionally struggles to maintain that. She loves her friends and attending church. She has reached her fourth stripe on her white belt in Brazilian jiujitsu, which is a much harder martial art to advance in than most martial arts.

Since she has trained in fighting, I wondered if she has ever been in a street fight. She said her dad only allows her to defend herself; so she can only fight if someone hits her first, and no one has.

I asked if she has ever been tempted to beat someone up who didn't punch her first. After a pause and a smile, she very softly replied, "Yeah." I knew the answer but was more interested in testing her honesty, and she unmistakably was shooting straight with me.

I asked her about her favorite moment with her dad. She said shooting a video of them lip-synching to "Hello" by her favorite singer Adele on her twelfth birthday. The video is on YouTube. I watched it along with thousands of other people, and it is a precious bonding moment.

The video of which she spoke was a hit on social media. This tenderhearted moment was shared over eight hundred times on Facebook and seen by more than a hundred thousand viewers. Raised by a dad who is always in the spotlight, Savannah seems braced for the attention of the public eye. It does not bother her that so many people watched her clowning around with her dad.

There is no doubting the sincere love between these two. Her admiration for Ivey is huge. His conviction to stop at nothing to take care of his little girl reveals his innermost character and great love for her. Ivey's Facebook album of Savannah says it all: "My daughter!!!!!!! :) :) :) My everything!!!!!"

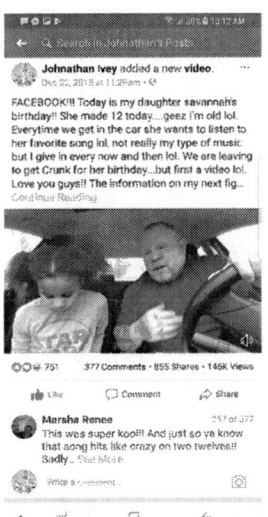

A clip from Ivey's Facebook page, where so many watched father and daughter do the music video. Celebrities brought this video up on their own when I interviewed them, saying what a great dad Ivey is.

Ivey dressed as a gorilla and Savannah as a banana for Halloween.

Savannah with her puppy, Tiger.

Savannah's first Halloween.

Savannah on her twelfth birthday.

Savannah right before watching her dad fight for the first time.

Savannah with her grandmother and her dad.

CHAPTER 7

# The Monster's Classic Battles

> The Lord will preserve him and keep him alive,
> And he will be blessed on the earth;
> You will not deliver him to the will of his enemies.
> —Psalm 41:2 (NKJV)

When a fighter takes on every opponent in his path, he accumulates a long list of matches in a hurry. Unless someone knows the mixed martial arts business, they do not realize the impact of not taking the time to recover before returning to competition. Ivey, of course, holds the record for the most fights in one year, but as I studied his career, it began to sink in how insane this was!

He and I were sitting in a restaurant one evening discussing the time he fought in three different states in nine days' time. I asked for his schedule for those nine days. After a few minutes pulling up stuff on his phone, he gave me the shocking list. In 2001, he was on a Bushido card in Arizona on January eighteenth. The next day, he traveled to Florida, where he fought on a Battle Jax card. Then he had exactly seven days to rest and recuperate before he went to Indiana to be on a Hook & Shoot card. I could not imagine this, and the facts sank in, in waves. Three fights in nine days!

As he told me this, I recalled the soreness and injuries after just amateur grappling. The last athletics I ever did was an exhibition grappling match against a cage fighter to help fill a gap in a card for Strike Out Promotions a few years ago. We were not allowed to strike each other, only wrestle. I won but got slammed into the cage once, and as a result of slipping out of a leg lock attempt, I pulled a lower leg muscle. The next day, I could barely move from the soreness; my lower leg had swelled up all the way to the knee, and I limped for six weeks! As I thought of this, I was in shock and awe over Ivey's packed schedule. How could he possibly function in the cage, sore, injured, and without any real recovery time, fighting deadly professionals as often as twice in the same weekend?

I commented about this during one discussion, and Ivey's reaction was to tell me of one busy weekend that stood out in his mind. He had fought on both Friday and Saturday nights, then traveled to a Sunday fight in which he missed a flight and was unable to make the third straight day! There were so many times he fought handicapped for various reasons. Sometimes he had to fight without punching his opponent back due to swollen hands from a previous battle. Other times it might be vision problems or muscular injury or any from an extensive list of possibilities. Short notice was another issue, often not having a clue who he would be fighting until the day of the event. But he always fought.

With a list of so many fights, does any stand out? Of course. It did not take long to decide we needed a whole chapter just to highlight some of these.

**Johnathan Ivey**    -Versus-    **Harry Moskowitz**

Out of all of Ivey's opponents, I would have to cast my vote for my favorite to be Harry Moskowitz! It was more than just a match—it was in many ways the dramatic conclusion of a journey for Ivey.

When Ivey became a fighter, MMA was still new, and he rented every video of the sport to study. He felt right about his journey—that is, until he watched a UFC video of Harry Moscowitz. Being short limbed and lacking height for his weight division, Ivey was concerned about taller opponents' considerable advantage of reach on him. Ivey saw six-foot-five-inch Harry, a striker who loves to ground his opponent and then pound them out, and for the very first time, he was intimidated. In fact, he almost backed out of pro fighting when he saw Harry in action. Harry became the one guy Ivey never wanted to face. He continued on and just thought he would avoid fighting Harry.

I had the pleasure of interviewing Harry. I would vote him not only as my favorite of Ivey's opponents, but also as my favorite personality of all those whom he fought! Harry is a great guy. He gladly gave me his cell phone number, told me to call anytime. It was not like a phone interview at all; we enjoyed talking, often getting off the topic of the discussion and rambling about the sport and life itself. He is the kind of guy who just enjoys life and is not wrapped up in his ego at all.

Harry, like Ivey, happened into the sport. He was a bouncer who threatened to remove a loud group of guys from the bar. One man at the table pointed out that it would be a mistake. Harry asked him if he had a few more guys in the restroom because he had no one at the table that worried him. The man doing the talking was impressed by Harry's confidence and explained he was putting on a cage fighting event that weekend and the guys at the table were fighters. He asked if Harry would be interested in fighting on the show, which Harry agreed to do. As they say "The rest is history."

Also like Ivey, Harry did some unsanctioned brawling for money. He did some bar challenges, where there was a ring in a bar, everyone put in fifty-dollars, and fought. At the end of the night, the last man standing got the pot. These challenges are illegal now; I am not sure they ever were legal. Today there are harsh penalties for unsanctioned events, but back in the day, it was not uncommon.

Harry said that when the UFC came to his area, he pestered Art Davey to let him on the card. He said it took about two weeks of nagging, and then a spot opened up. Harry became known to the world at that point.

Both Ivey and Harry are real warriors. Guys who had a lot of rough talent and just fought whoever was in their paths, instead of being like too many who pick and choose to baby-step to a record that was better than they were.

Though Ivey planned never to fight Harry, fate doesn't work that way. As a single dad needing money, Ivey was taking every fight he could to make ends meet: then came the shocking offer to fight who? Of course, it was Harry Moskowitz! His mind returned to the UFC video, and he was scared to death. However, he needed the money to provide for his baby girl, so he had to take the offer to fight the man who was more frightening to him than any other.

Harry likes to go right to work brawling, and Ivey always attempts to finish fast, mostly for his nervousness. This fight was destined to be a short war. As soon as the referee began the match, they went at it hard. Harry was prepared to slug it out to the finish, and Ivey appeared to be going along with that plan as well, and then suddenly pulled Harry to the ground on top of him and landed in a quick leg lock. More important than a win or loss was facing his biggest fear, and he had.

When Harry recalls the match, he laughs about the loss. He said he just didn't see it coming; Ivey's speed caught him off guard. Harry could feel his knee was going to break, so to avoid permanent damage, Harry tapped out. He is a sportsman; he had no ill will about the loss at all.

When I asked him about Ivey, Harry said he was impressed with Ivey in and out of the ring. He listed off many qualities he liked about Ivey and had nothing unfavorable to say about him. Like most everyone who knows Ivey, Harry mentioned Ivey's humility, conviction, and parenting. Harry had recently recommended Ivey to a promoter as a great fighter they should consider matching.

# JOHNATHAN IVEY: THE MAN BEHIND THE MONSTER

**Johnathan Ivey**   -Versus-   **Dan "the Beast" Severn**

Two of the best-known names Ivey ever faced were two UFC Hall of Fame fighters: Ken Shamrock and Dan Severn. I mention both together because of the similarities of the situation. Ivey was never allowed in the UFC; there are only rumors as to why. It would hurt the quality of Ivey's biography to mention hearsay, so I will not.

Ivey speaks well of Dan Severn, saying he was a great guy. They talked after the fight, and he impressed Ivey with his lack of ego. Severn had earned his reputation; one online source said he had one hundred and one wins recorded. Many fights never make the records so there is no telling what his true career totals could be.

I diligently sought a video of the matchup but found none. The online records recorded the results. For some reason, it was one of those fights that avoided video, to the best of my knowledge. The match was in a ring, like pro wrestling, it was not cage fighting, but the rules were the same.

The rivalry was hard to predict in that both men needed the fight on the ground, each on their terms. However, in the minds of most, it was a legend against just another fighter. Dan was a world-class wrestler who wanted to put Ivey on his back. Ivey was a ground-fighting submission artist who needed access to Dan's legs. They both had their work cut out for them; this would not be yet another easy win for Dan Severn.

The action soon revealed that Dan Severn could not manhandle Ivey, who was way too overpowering for him to take down. This fact gave Ivey a confidence boost. To the surprise of many, Ivey, who began the sport as an untrained thug off the street, was holding his own against the wrestling legend.

In the second round, the two athletes stood and threw punches until Ivey caught Dan with a left hook that sent him crashing to the mat. Ivey put Severn in a kneebar, but time ran out, and the round ended, saving Severn. The contest remained in limbo until it went to the judges for a decision. The judges gave the nod to Dan Severn.

It was a disappointment for Ivey. He says concerning this fight, "Everyone always says I should have won, but I won that fight." Ivey has gone the distance with many fighters, but I don't recall any other time he claimed he should have received the decision. Since I did not see the video, all I can say is, my experience is Ivey tells it like it is and doesn't make excuses.

It is true that judges don't like Ivey's style—that is no secret. Also, judges sometimes recognize reputations in close matchups. What if you're the odd judge out who says a nobody beat a legend in a split decision? Would it cause you not to be asked to judge again? I wish the video were available so the readers could make their call on this one.

In some ways, this was an impressive victory for Ivey. Many times he was dismissed as a joke, yet once again, he had proven he could hold his own on the level of some of the sport's greatest athletes. When everyone thinks a matchup will be a slaughter and it ends up a judge's decision, that speaks for itself.

I finally managed to track down and interview, Dan "The Beast" Severn. I found Dan is not the low intellect brute many have portrayed him to be. He is a highly intelligent business wizard with over four decades of astounding accomplishments in multiple sports as well as other areas of life. His impressive level of humility does not stop him from approaching everything he does with the same intensity with which he fights.

I asked Dan to share his thoughts about the fight with Ivey. Dan explained he fought too many matches to recall all of them.

## JOHNATHAN IVEY: THE MAN BEHIND THE MONSTER

"I honestly don't remember anything about fighting him, but I must have won because I never forget when I lose," Dan said laughing.

**Johnathan Ivey**     -Versus-     **Ken Shamrock**

In time, he was offered a fight against Ken Shamrock, who was Dan Severn's old nemesis and fellow UFC Hall of Famer. This matchup was not as much of a clash of styles as the Dan Severn matchup. Both Ivey and Shamrock held respected reputations for their leg locks. I remember everyone from my gym talking about this match; it was thought to be the Battle of the Leg Locks.

In this matchup, Shamrock surprised many by avoiding the ground. The intelligent Shamrock is known for studying his opponents well before a fight. It is not a secret; takedowns are one of the weaker points of Ivey's game. Shamrock attempted to force Ivey to burn his energy to take him down. It did not make the intense ground battle everyone had hoped for, but Shamrock is known to come in with the best game plan to win. His best hope to beat Ivey was to avoid grappling.

The match passed with mostly stand-up fighting from two men, who don't stand up much while fighting. Ironically, Ivey knocked Shamrock down in the second round by a left hook. The same round and punch had knocked down Dan Severn. The fight ended with the same results—a decision win against Ivey.

I watched a video of both the fight and the postfight interview with Ken Shamrock. In the interview, Ken acknowledged he wanted to avoid grappling with Ivey. I took this as a significant compliment from the UFC legend.

Ivey made no claims the decision should have been for him. He showed me out-of-character things in the video that he was doing out of pure nervousness in this fight. He was under a ton of pressure; Ivey mentioned he kept thinking, *I am in here with Ken Shamrock!* In a repetitive story, a single dad trying to provide for his little girl had climbed in the cage with one of the world's top fighters and held his own.

I had an interview lined up with Ken Shamrock, but unfortunately, his people contacted me to say he would have to reschedule, and that never happened. I would love to hear Shamrock's opinion of Ivey. So far, I have not found any who speak ill of him once they have fought.

The saddest part of this matchup for me was the disrespect Ivey received, not from his opponent, but from others. A former UFC champion commented laughing at an attempted rolling kneebar by Ivey. He claimed he had no idea what Ivey was trying to do. I find it hard to imagine that anyone could be a UFC champion and not know that move, considering I have seen it used in the UFC. The technique failed to work because the sly Shamrock did not fall for the trick move, so Ivey did a double summersault to put distance between him and his opponent until he could get back to his feet. That former champ lost me as a fan the day I heard him make his biased statements that were so disrespectful and degrading.

Ivey also mentioned another upsetting bias in this fight. He said that in some videos, the film was edited, taking things that happened in two different rounds and putting them together to make him look bad. He mentioned that in one case where he beats his chest in a challenge to Shamrock, the film is cut and shows a Shamrock highlight that happened in another round, as though Ivey was humiliated by his provocation receiving an instant reckoning. Sadly, we live in such a world of technology that we may no longer believe what we see sometimes.

**Johnathan Ivey   -Versus-   Sean McCorkle**

UFC vet Sean McCorkle and Ivey are friends now. They even vacationed together once. Sean was quick to respond when I asked him for an interview, and I found he knows Ivey well. He spoke highly of Ivey as a fighter, a person, and, especially, a father.

Sean gave me this quote: "I'd just say that Ivey has never gotten the real respect he deserves as a fighter. Had he had a good manager from the very beginning of his career, there is no telling where he might have ended up. Not that he has anything to be ashamed of, but when you're forced financially to take bad matchups on really short notice, it can really mess up your record pretty quickly."

Sean knows all too well about this dilemma. He had an incredible record of nineteen and two until he had a devastating back injury. Facing the need to retire, he did not have the finances, so he fought hurt, resulting in losing five of his last six fights. The fight business is as cruel as nature's food chain.

This match with McCorkle and Ivey was different in that instead of Ivey facing a legend from the UFC, Sean needed to fight Ivey to get into the UFC. Sean was not afraid to go on record and call

Ivey "the gateway to the UFC." He explained to me that if you could get a win against Ivey, the UFC would sign you.

This situation indicated Ivey was not overlooked by the UFC, but was avoided for some reason. I have been a matchmaker, and I know about preferences, types I avoided for various reasons. I always avoided undependable ones who often pull out or cancel, but that is not Ivey. Another category I dodged was those who were a liability risk, pulling dangerous, dirty tricks, like targeting the spine or using eye pokes. It is the matchmaker's right to recruit whom they please, but I will always wonder why Ivey was never a consideration for the UFC in his prime.

Sean McCorkle was the kind of fighter Ivey should have avoided, and probably would have if he would have had a manager calling the shots. Every fighter has that one type of opponent who can exploit their weaknesses, and McCorkle was precisely that. Ivey has short limbs, which is a weak point against the reach advantage of much taller opponents.

Ivey knew this was to be a struggle. Sean was approximately close to a foot taller than him and had a classic sprawl that made him a challenge to take down. This advantage was terrible for Ivey, potentially stopping him from every move he frequently does.

The various sources I checked on Sean's height had him listed at six foot seven up to six foot ten. Catching the discrepancies in profiles after my interview made me regret I did not get the chance to ask him his height. I sent Sean a Facebook message asking which height was accurate, and within a few minutes, a joking response came saying that it depends on whether he is standing up or lying down.

Sean studied Ivey and came up with a game plan of using his superior size to his advantage. The strategy was to force Ivey to the ground and to trap him on all fours with his inside shin pinning Ivey's Achilles tendon to the mat. Then finish Ivey from the disabled position with strikes.

Sean had an excellent plan, and it worked almost flawlessly. In Sean's interview, he said the only thing that went wrong was that he underestimated how hard Ivey was to hurt. He explained that when it came to the strikes, Ivey can take an incredible amount of damage. A friend of Sean's reviewed the footage and said Sean hit Ivey two hundred and seventy-six times! At one point, Ivey looked up at the referee and calmly said, "Don't stop it, I am fine."

Sean said, "I remember being shocked he would not quit, no matter how many times I hit him." McCorkle suffered injured hands that caused him pain for weeks. He was sure he had several small fractures in both fists. Despite Ivey's protest, the referee did eventually choose to call the fight.

Sean was then allowed to fight his next match in the UFC, as he had predicted. The UFC gave him an underdog match against Mark Hunt, which he was expected to lose. He broke Mark Hunt's arm with an armbar in the first round. Ivey had presented considerably more challenge than Sean's UFC competitor, though Sean did stress how hard Mark Hunt could hit!

Later in his career, McCorkle trained grappling with Johnathan Ivey, but was unable to do much due to the back injury. Praising Ivey's ground skills, he regretted not being able to spar with him earlier in his career. He noted that fellow UFC vet Jake O'Brien had said he was shocked by Ivey's grappling skills, remarking that Jake had only ever said that about just two people ever.

**Johnathan Ivey**   -Versus-   **Ricco Rodriguez**

Ricco won the UFC heavyweight title by beating one of the all-time greats of MMA, Randy Couture. That alone makes this man stand out more than anything else. Eventually, Ivey was matched with Ricco outside of the UFC, in Houston, Texas.

Ivey admits he had a bad plan in this fight. He was too interested in proving the devastating fighter that had taken out Randy Couture could not hurt him. For Ivey, this is the typical behavior that crowds love but does not impress judges. Ivey dropped his hands and challenged Ricco to knock him out. Ricco could not do so. Unable to knock Ivey out, Ricco trapped Ivey against the cage and controlled him for yet another time Ivey went the distance with a top UFC veteran.

One classic moment in this fight was when Ivey was entertaining the crowd with his crane technique from the movie *Karate Kid*. The move is better known as the Karate Kid Kick. The kick is never considered a threat because the stance of holding one knee up in the air and the hands above the head will flag your opponent to precisely what you are going to do—a jumping front snap karate kick. The movie technique based on speed and agility is especially nonthreatening from a heavyweight fighter with a low center of gravity in his physique. It also requires the target to walk right into the line of fire, as happened in the movie. Ricco aggressed confidently against the clowning Ivey, and Ivey landed the kick! Ivey now laughs and admits he might be the first fighter in history to make that move work.

Ivey threatens with a *Karate Kid* crane kick to entertain the crowd.

## JOHNATHAN IVEY: THE MAN BEHIND THE MONSTER

Johnathan Ivey    -Versus-    Robert Villegas

On my trip to Kokomo, Indiana (the location of Ivey's upcoming title fight), I met Ivey's boxing coach for the first time. I got a chance to ask him about times he trained Ivey for a fight and cornered for him. When I asked Fred about memorable experiences with Ivey, he had plenty, but one stood out considerably. He had worked with Ivey when Ivy fought Robert Villegas.

This matchup is significant because it reveals how Ivey gains such loyal supporters. The matchup took place in Corpus Christi, Texas, where the hometown crowd was clearly for Villegas and was for the Extreme Combat Heavy Weight Championship which took place on the Blood & Glory card. Ivey was an underdog, and that put tons of pressure on Villegas to do well.

The much taller Villegas was very talented and knew to avoid the ground with Ivey. Fred described the match as Villegas consistently backpedaling to avoid committing to taking on Ivey. MMA fans tend to hate this.

Villegas was consistently jabbing with his reach advantage as he backed away to keep Ivey from reaching him. Ivey has had so many fights that he bleeds very easily due to scar tissue around his eyes. The results of Villegas's jabs were a severe cut around his eye.

Frustrated by his opponent running from him, Ivey became vocal, yelling at his opponent, and even at his opponent's cornermen. He chased his opponent the whole fight, beating his chest and yelling, "Fight me!" When I watched the highlights, I was shocked. Villegas was a beast of a man, but he looked scared as he ran back from the bloody Ivey as he was shouting.

The judges ruled the contest a unanimous decision against Ivey. Ivey was taking jabs as Villegas backpedaled, which does score points. A strategic win for Villegas, but the choice of strategy was not a fan-winning one. Ivey's style of fight to finish rarely ever gains him a decision victory, but it is what the fans like to see.

The crowd, who were fans of Villegas's at the start, now booed loudly at the decision. When the enraged Ivey exited, a large group of former Villegas fans surrounded the path Ivey traveled back to the locker room chanting "Ivey! Ivey!"

Fred's story told it all. Ivey does not have a perfect record, but he has the hearts of his supporters. He does not seek to steal wins by points but to fight until someone wins outright. The crowd from Villegas's hometown seemed to agree. After the fight, Ivey signed autographs and posed for pictures with children. The same people who had first cheered against him now loved him. Despite the loss, Ivey was inspired to see he had won over a crowd.

**Johnathan Ivey** -Versus- **Joe Nameth**

Nameth is not to be confused with Joe Namath the football legend, as this is a different person. Nameth was not one of the Hall of Fame legends Ivey fought, but it was a significant fight for several reasons. The two fought twice, actually. If you watch the first meeting online, you can see why Nameth would want a rematch. When a fight ends too fast, people often think it was a fluke win, and sometimes it is; and after the rematch, you know for sure.

On their first encounter, Ivey, a grappler, won by knockout in only eight seconds. No one could see that coming, except, of course, Ivey. I found an old article written before the fight, giving Ivey a slight advantage over Nameth. The expert predicted Ivey had a 68 percent chance of victory but stated it was unlikely he would win by knockout. Ivey got described as having weak knockout abilities.

Ivey does, in fact, hit extremely hard; he is just better at grappling. Nameth went crashing down on the first punch, and Ivey followed up with a few quick strikes on the ground before the referee stopped the fight. From the video, it appears to me that Nameth was out cold when he went down after the first punch.

After about two years, the pair rematched. I was unable to find a video of the rematch, and there was very little media coverage other than to say Ivey won again. There are, however, highlights from the rematch on some of Ivey's videos showing off his impressive flashy pro wrestling–style moves that the crowds seem to love but judges and critics hate.

During this match, he knocked Nameth down and then performed the pro wrestling move often referred to as the People's Elbow. Pro wrestlers usually jump into the air, dropping all their body weight down into an elbow strike to their downed opponent. The move is, of course, faked in pro wrestling.

A pro wrestler explained to me that he had trained with Styrofoam cups, which they set on the mat for target practice. The idea is to dent the cup barely. If you can dent but not crush it, you can drop the elbow on your opponent safely. This move will look real and impress the crowd, without hurting your opponent.

Ivey does not train with Styrofoam cups, nor does he execute fake moves, but he loves to entertain the crowd. He did a real pro wrestling–style elbow drop on Joe Nameth after knocking him down! I can only imagine Ivey's elbow backed by his dense body weight crushing down on me! Ivey won the rematch, but he gained more fame from the pro wrestling–style antics than the win.

**Roy Jones Jr**
Sep 1 at 11:34am

He may have never made it into the UFC but Jonathan Ivey is one of the biggest names around. With over 100 Professional MMA fights, Crazy walkout entrances and the most Leglock victories in MMA history, Ivey is one of the most entertaining fighters we've ever seen. We're glad to have him be apart of our events! Check out the "Leglock Monster's" Highlight reel!

**Johnathan "The Leglock Monster" Ivey (Highlight Reel) - FIGHT...**
fightbananas.com

938 likes   42 comments

 Like     Comment     Share

Six-time World Champion brags on the Leg Lock Monster.

CHAPTER 8

# The Bad Apple

For all have sinned and come short of the glory of GOD.
—Romans 3:23 (NKJV)

One of my memorable moments with Ivey was when he admitted he has not always been a Christian man. He soberly said, "For about fifteen of my adult years, I was a bad apple." There was a short pause. "Well, okay, twenty."

We often talked of those years. Ivey spoke of the potential destruction he escaped year after year, and of the regrets he now holds.

I wanted to set aside one chapter to highlight some of them.

Ivey's goal for the biography was that it would tell all, good and bad. He is a bit of a closed book with people, only occasionally opening up to social media. With me, he has been very forthright about his dark past, openly admitting many mistakes and regrets in his life.

As both a Christian counselor and a minister, I have come to appreciate genuine regret and honesty about one's sinful past. More commonly today, people blame their behavior on others to avoid personal responsibility. Ivey was astonishingly open about this topic, making me understand his willingness to agree to a tell-all biography.

Conversion is considered by many a complicated church word, but it just means a reversal or change in character. Church pews are full of people who gain false confidence in who they are, boasting of what they have never done instead of examining what God has helped them to overcome. Real religion has the power to change people, not keep them the same. Ivey has changed, and that change is real. He is still a bit rough around the edges, but aren't we all? Some just hide it better than others.

Ivey's sincere hope is that readers of this book may be positively affected by their relationship with God. What will appear in this chapter is not things Ivey is proud of, but things that he is thankfully blessed to overcome. He knows many people out there are struggling with a less-than-ideal start in life as he did. It takes help from God to make it. Ivey has learned that and wanted it for others.

The various scandals selected for this chapter were each chosen for a reason. My personal favorite was an act of violence with a humorous twist. I suppose this one reveals my twisted sense of humor, but I could not stop laughing as Ivey explained it to me.

Ivey has a bit of a personal pet peeve when it comes to road rage and takes horn blowing as a personal insult. He says horn blowing is like bullying or asserting authority over someone. That one particular rub has resulted in many of his altercations. I never thought of it that way, but it makes sense.

One day, driving through Clarksville, Ivey was driving a little too fast, and a man in his car with his wife blew his horn at him. When the man and Ivey both pulled into a parking lot, the angry man rushed up to Ivey and began yelling. Ivey instantly knocked the man unconscious with a single punch.

The man's wife began screaming for someone to call the police, so Ivey left the scene. Someone got his license plate number, resulting in his arrest a few days later. The entire incident was caught on security cameras since it took place in the parking lot of a Target department store.

When the court date came, Ivey learned the detailed irony of this episode. The man was a commanding officer at Fort Campbell. Since Ivey shaved his head and had a lot of muscle, he looked very much like a soldier. The commander was planning to scold what he thought was a soldier under his command for displaying poor driving skills in public. He was unaware he was aggressing upon a cage fighting legend who was offended by the mistreatment. Ivey was court ordered into anger management but served no time.

The local newspaper wrote an article detailing the identity of both men and the irony of the incident. The reporter took a humorous jab at the story. The report concluded that the commanding officer would not likely be blowing his horn at anyone again anytime soon.

Ivey had, in fact, lived a hard life during his bad years, but his arrests don't include anything else except assault. However, his record has nearly two dozen arrests for this one crime. He is a fighter, and as he says, "It's all I know how to do. Ninety-nine percent of people run away from fights, but 1 percent of us run to them." Fighters often know no other way to deal with things.

A close second on my list of favorites would be a mere verbal confrontation that got heated and later resulted in a brawl. The situation was sad and regrettable all around, but the reason I note this one is not because of what happened but, rather, *when* it took place. Ivey was going to his court-ordered anger management when an SUV full of people did the unspeakable: they blew their horn at him. So ironically he confronted them on his way to anger management!

Ivey, as always, pulled in for the confrontation, only to find they were all females. There was no fight due to their gender, but the verbal confrontation got out of control, and the police came. The women lied to the police and accused him of racial hatred since they were black, claiming he was using the n-word on them. Ivey would never do that. His daughter was black; he spent the later years of his youth in an all-black home and had many black friends, one of whom was his roommate at the time. The women did not know this; it was just a convenient lie.

The policeman did not arrest anyone because there was no proof, only word of mouth. However, the police took Ivey's name and address and gave it to the women, informing them they could go file a complaint if they thought they had a case. The women did not submit anything but stirred up tensions and arranged for Ivey to be attacked by a gang of five men at his home shortly after this.

A few days later, there was a knock at Ivey's door. When he opened the door, he saw one large black man that he did not recognize. The man asked for Ivey by his full name. Ivey was immediately suspicious. He glanced outside, spotting two more men hiding to the left of the door and another two on the right. Ivey's first guess was this was the residue from the episode where the policeman gave his address to the women in the SUV. The four additional men appeared to be average in size. Still, the odds were five to one. Ivey had a gun in the house, but the men appeared to be unarmed, so he walked out to confront them, feeling he could take them if there were no weapons involved.

Ivey saw one of the four smaller men hand a retractable baton to the big man. A fight broke out, and Ivey was clubbed across the head, causing significant bleeding; but he was still not hurt badly enough to slow him down. He took the armed man to the ground, beating him while his four friends punched and kicked Ivey, but doing only minimal damage.

Despite the help of his attacker's friends Ivey used an ankle lock to disable him. The fight was disrupted when Ivey's roommate walked outside and fired his gun in the air, scattering the four smaller men. They fled to their car and abandoned their fallen friend.

Witnesses had called the police. When the police arrived, Ivey said that he did not wish to press charges, and he asked them to leave. Ivey never calls the police; it's a personal rule of his.

The witnesses who had seen what happened, however, talked to the police. After the officers searched the area, they found the wounded man lying in a trench at a nearby construction site with a broken ankle, resulting from Ivey's lock. As it turned out, the attacker was a convicted armed robber and a recent parolee. They arrested him.

Johnathan Ivey was subpoenaed but did not show up for the court. He was not willing to testify. The attacker claimed to be a victim of assault and told the court how Ivey had broken his ankle. He could not justify why he was at Ivey's home when this happened, and he returned to prison for parole violation to complete his original sentencing.

Not all of Ivey's assaults involved the police; in fact, many times, he never heard from them again. One great regret was not the result of anger but a broken heart. Ivey, in his younger years, had a crush on a girl who rejected him. He was hurt and depressed. I know from being an MMA coach that fighters are dangerous when emotional. The smartest thing they can do is work out aggression in the gym to stay out of trouble. The dumbest thing they can do is go out in public because they always get in trouble.

Ivey turned to his friends and asked them to take him out on the town so he could find a fight to release some aggression. While out, they spotted three young men with a girl. He never offered a word; he just started the fight. Sadly, when Ivey attacked the first one, the others did not help; instead, they abandoned their friend and ran. Ivey busted the young man up badly while pinning him to the pavement by putting his knee on the boy's chest. His friends got him to leave to avoid arrest, and they never heard another word about that night. He regrets that fight to this day.

On his long list of assaults, he once beat up a man who ran the go-carts at a fun center. His friends were bumping each other with the carts. The man told them they had to leave, but they had already paid for the next ride. He would not refund their money. A verbal conflict heated up between the man and Ivey, and again, Ivey knocked yet another stranger out with a single punch. He left to avoid arrest but punched a canopy on the way out, knocking it over. Some of the witnesses recognized Ivey and told the police he was a professional fighter. The police tracked him down. Ivey received extended probation time.

Ivey got arrested for assault almost two dozen times. He avoided law far more times than that. He had only done jail time once. At age eighteen, he was sentenced to thirty days. Since then, he seemed charmed to escape. Each assault ended with no charges or was pleaded down to a misdemeanor with no time behind bars.

Few are as fortunate, as police and judges tend to take a trained fighter, especially a professional one, as armed, as if they had a weapon. Another pro fighter friend of mine was attacked from behind and clubbed over the head. He responded in self-defense and beat his attacker nearly to death; he was forced to spend eight months in jail, despite his attacker being armed. Somehow Ivey always escaped the pro fighter prejudice. He beat the system nearly two dozen times.

One essential mile marker in his life was when that luck ran out. His last and final arrest was a turning point. In this case, he got viewed as a pro fighter who had hurt a victim instead of just a brawler.

Being a social drinker, he restricted his drinking to when he was with friends. On this one night, he had way too much alcohol, more than doubling what it would take to intoxicate him. Once the two friends had consumed twenty-six mixed drinks, they were asked to leave the Mexican restaurant. Departing and going to another location, they drank even more.

Shortly after this, someone began to provoke him to the point of rage, with hurtful statements. Ivey, still under the effects of extreme intoxication, became violent and was unaware of his actions. The resulting charges were much more severe than in the past.

When the police came to his home, he resisted arrest, not wanting to leave a young Savannah alone while she slept. The policemen, sizing him up, called twelve additional officers for backup. Later, when he and the police reached better terms, they informed him twelve backup officers called for backup was a new record!

He explained his motive, and they peacefully agreed to allow him to find someone to stay with Savannah before taking him. The officers seemed to respect the fatherly instinct to have his daughter's well-being as the priority. The situation calmed, and they began to sense this was not an average arrestee they were dealing with, in more ways than one.

When they attempted to handcuff Ivey, they found that his shoulders were too broad for his short limbs. It was impossible to make is hands meet behind his back because his arms could not reach each other. Ivey was cooperative and well mannered, presenting no threat of danger. The police decided to take him without having his hands restrained behind him.

Once the officers figured out who he was, they were impressed with his mellow behavior now that he was sober. They watched his videos on YouTube and spoke with him about his fights.

He was not as fortunate with the courts. This time the prosecution went after Ivey with a vengeance. The plea deal they offered was six years in prison. He would miss seeing his daughter Savannah grow up if he were convicted. He stalled and negotiated as the trial date came nearer, but the district attorney did not budge. It appeared a lengthy sentence was unavoidable.

Fortune blessed him once more when jailers, officers, a probation officer, and his minister all came to his defense on how well mannered he was. The overwhelming number of respectable character witnesses was causing the courts to lose confidence in the slam-dunk conviction they had planned. In response, Ivey was given a new plea deal, thirty days in jail and two years probation. Additionally, if he were to get in any trouble during the two years, he must complete the full six years behind bars.

As a result, Ivey never drank again. He could not take a chance on getting in any trouble, or he would surely lose his daughter. This turning point was the final step, leading him to a conservative Christian lifestyle. Some would now say he is a dull stay-at-home dad compared to who he once was. He busies himself with training for fights and taking care of Savannah. His social life is very carefully chosen to avoid trouble and limited to a selective group of friends.

Ivey was anxious to do his thirty days and get on with life. He arrived at the jail and went through the degrading process of becoming an inmate. He determined to avoid any problems while on the inside that might prolong his sentence for any unacceptable behavior.

No sooner had Ivey entered his cell than he was approached by a white supremacist prison gang. In this particular institution, the dominant force was that group with a powerful reputation. Ivey described them as a modern version of the Ku Klux Klan. Similarly, an Internet news article referred to the group as a type of more liberal Nazi extremist.

They filled Ivey's cell with their numbers and then attempted to recruit him. Ivey explained that he was there for thirty days and interested only in peacefully doing his time and getting out. The gang accepted his answer and exited.

Following the white supremacist departing from his cell was a large number from another group, this time all black. They questioned Ivey about his connection to the white supremacists and his intentions. He gave the same answers.

The first two days, it would appear he was going to have a hard time avoiding trouble on the inside. By the third day, the word got out of who he was. He spent his time, teaching MMA from within his cell since the commons area had security cameras. Ivey got along well with both inmates and jailers. As he hoped, his sentence ended without incident, and he went home, aspiring to be done with the rough life forever.

The list of regrets and bad experiences is long, indeed, but his worst mistake, fortunately, is the one that never happened. In Ivey's younger years, he decided to do a drive-by shooting, which would have been the biggest mistake of his entire life. Instead, that night is an addition to his long list of near misses that he reflects back on.

Ivey and three of his friends drove a few towns over to Lincoln City. His friends were wearing bandanas. They drove past two guys walking down the road, who reacted to them offensively making gestures with their hands.

Ivey's group decided to turn around and go back to confront the two. However, the two entered a house. So Ivey and his friends traveled on to a store where two of his group went in with the intent to steal some alcohol.

While they were in the store, a gang of about thirty guys in five cars pulled up and got out with baseball bats. Ivey attempted to run through the crowd with the car but got hung up on a barrier. While the car was stuck, the gang began to hammer the car with their bats.

Finally getting the car loose, Ivey drove it down some side roads to lose the gang, after which he doubled back to pick up the two friends in the store. The two had come out and been looking for the car, unaware of what had taken place.

Angered, the group decided to go home to get guns and then come back to do a drive by on the house that the first two gang members had entered that same night. It was at this time that good fortune unfolded. The car broke down, preventing the planned drive-by.

He has mentioned that many times, thinking back as to how bad his life could have been if the car had not broken down. Where would he be now? He had beaten the odds many times, but he never wants to be that person again.

When people look at their mistakes and regret them, it is called repentance. That is the key to change. Without it, people never correct themselves. It is a quality everyone needs, not just Ivey. Jesus said, "Unless you repent you will all likewise perish" (Luke 13:3).

Ivey is a bit rough around the edges still in any Christian's eye. He still struggles with many things. However, few churchgoers will ever overcome as much as Ivey already has in the first half of his volatile life. He is still far from perfect, but then again aren't we all?

A self-described unsaved twenty-year-old Johnathan Ivey.

Ivey after being saved.

CHAPTER 9

# Romancing the Monster

*Who can find a virtuous wife? For her worth is far above rubies.*
—Proverbs 31:10 (NKJV)

Not surprisingly, Ivey's love life is complicated. With his life and career, it would be hard to imagine a smooth-running romantic life, but he dreams of having a blissful union with a trusted wife someday. He insists his wife must be a role model for his daughter and is reluctant to introduce dates to Savannah until he thinks she may be that potential wife and mother.

Ivey was married once many years ago to Savannah's mom. Everyone who sees Savannah is curious. She is, of course, interracial. The beautiful little girl has light black skin and adorably cute "Afro-puffs" as Ivey and his barber Michael Weems call her hairstyle, which is two balls separated like pigtails.

Ivey, on the other hand, has light white skin. To quote Ivey's black barber from his hilarious interview about Ivey, "Besides the ink, he doesn't got a lot of pigment." The color clash between Ivey's daughter and himself draws much attention from everyone. It is rare to see a snow-white single dad with a little black girl, and that attracts a lot of questions from curious people. The interracial marriage to Savannah's mom was short, but the race was never an issue.

Ivey married after he found out he was going to be a father. He was prepared to commit to a more conservative family lifestyle for Savannah's sake; his wife was not yet ready for that much change. A classic problem when couples try to settle down is that one is more inclined than the other. Problems set in right away as a result.

When the couple decided to split, at first it was Ivey who would depart alone. He was gone only a matter of hours before deciding he could not live without Savannah. He returned to his wife with a suggestion: since he was the one who wanted to settle into a family life, perhaps it would be better if Savannah went with him. Surprisingly, they agreed, and Ivey began his learning experience as the clueless single dad whose only skill was fighting. Beating the odds, he has done it well.

That was Ivey's first attempt at marriage, and some of his attempts at dating have gone much worse. I asked him about his worst experiences. He told me a shocking story of a woman who I will refer to only as Catfish. He calls this frightening story the time he got catfished.

Ivey has by most people's observation, the bad boy look. We have all met girls who are hooked on the bad boys. As a Christian counselor, I have encountered too many self-destructive young ladies who waste exceptional potential pursuing one bad boy after another. One girl once told me the perfect man is Captain Jack Sparrow from the movie *Pirates of the Caribbean*. My response was, "You mean Johnny Depp, the actor who played the part?" She stressed that she did not want Depp; she wanted the exact pirate, Captain Jack Sparrow. Like moths drawn to a flame, they cannot help themselves. Put bluntly, the bad boy is what turns them on.

This complication is one noticeable weakness in Ivey's pursuit of his soul mate. Women who like the bad boy will likely be disappointed to find out that with Ivey, they are getting a good guy—he just doesn't look the part. Those who seek a good guy will likely never give him a second look because Ivey's appearance sends the wrong signals.

So many I have interviewed spoke concerning Ivey, "Don't judge a book by its cover." Most all agree his appearance is misleading to his character. I once heard a beautiful woman say, "I want a good guy who looks but doesn't act like the bad boy." I wish I could go back and find her for Johnathan Ivey.

There is also another type of girl, ones like Catfish, who do not have excellent potential and are dangerous to the men. Men can be victims too, especially when they are in love with a bad girl. The Bible speaks plainly of males led to their destruction by these types of women: "Immediately he went after her, as an ox goes to the slaughter" (Prov. 7:22, NKJV).

Ivey encountered one of these danger girls drawn to his bad boy image. Catfish and Ivey met online. That one phrase "met online" often spells trouble, but I have met happy couples who met online. They are the exceptions, however, not the rule. Ivey's comfort zone is social media, as he can control the distance he allows people. Sadly, with that remoteness comes lack of knowledge and that is what made him vulnerable to Catfish.

Catfish seemed promising at first, and they hit it off. Catfish's mother became friends with him on Facebook too, and soon it looked like Ivey could fit in, in this loving family he had met. They soon started dating despite it being a long-distance relationship. At first, all was well, but Ivey's suspicions soon arose.

Eventually, he began to spot too much men's stuff in her house. She explained it away by only saying, "It was my ex-husband's. He never came back to get it." Ivey can overlook much in a relationship, but lying is a big pet peeve of his. He could prove nothing, but his gut instinct said this woman was lying to him. He ended the relationship.

Not long after the breakup, he was contacted by Catfish's mother on Facebook. She sent a picture of her daughter's smashed SUV. The mother said her daughter had attempted suicide in her grief over the breakup by deliberately crashing her SUV into an 18-wheeler. She said that her daughter had survived, but was in critical care in the hospital.

Ivey, who was responding with grief and guilt, prepared to see Catfish at the hospital. However, this elaborately planned hoax unraveled. She was not in the hospital, nor was she ever. There was no suicide attempt. She was still driving her SUV; she had taken a picture of a wrecked SUV from the Internet. In fact, Ivey was not even friends with her mother online; his stalker Catfish was pretending to be both mother and daughter since Ivey was family oriented. The man's stuff in the home was her husband's belongings. He traveled in his work and was unaware of his wife's deceptive online adventures.

Ivey already had trust issues, and this experience did not help him overcome those at all. He was prepared to accept almost anything as a concession, if only he could have an honest woman. He had attempted this trade-off in another relationship, and it did not go well.

Ivey dated a young lady with a drug problem. She was honest about it, and he saw that honesty as potential. As he explained, the girl was not exactly a real girlfriend. She was more of a friend whom he was there for, but she had girlfriend potential. I would not have understood that had I not had a few of those myself. I define them as girls we like but wisely fear to date.

This story had a sad ending as well, as too often happens in such cases. The girl was on parole and failed her drug test. She returned to complete her time behind bars, ending the brief relationship.

There was another troubled young woman that Ivey dated, which ended in even worse tragedy. He doesn't like to talk about this one; it is too painful. Available details are fewer. He did eventually tell me that she was unfaithful, and they broke up, and she later died of a heroin overdose. A short story, as well as a sad one.

Those who have tried to save people from themselves have often learned the hard way that it is an honorable cause with a discouragingly low rate of success. The attempts at this are painful, and the happy endings are mostly in fiction novels.

With all the dark clouds of poor matchups, I had to ask if there was one who got away. Ivey was solemn and knew who she was without pondering the question. "Ramona," he said with total certainty. She was the daughter of some of his closest friends, the Chandlers. Ramona was considerably younger than Ivey, but they made a good couple. After a little bit of a shaky ice-breaking process with her family, they loved him, and Ivey grew close with all the Chandlers.

Ramona appeared to be the one. He still loves the whole family to this day. In fact, their names are all tattooed around Ivey's neck, and he has no regret for that decision. The couple broke up over a single argument over "something stupid." Ivey quickly regretted breaking up with her and tried to reconcile, but Ramona refused to get back together.

By chance, I had met Ramona's sister at Ivey's first MMA show. She was cage side, and I mistook her for a fan sneaking into the restricted zone for officials only. I confronted her and asked who she was. "I am Johnathan's sister," she replied. I never questioned it due to her confidence.

Later, it hit me that Ivey was an only child. I brushed it off as perhaps a later-life stepsister, but one day the topic came up in conversation with Ivey. He looked puzzled at first and pondered it. Finally, he said, "Oh, that was Ramona's little sister, Bayleigh. She still calls me her big brother." As a big brother, Ivey had loaned the sister money for a car, and she had paid back every dollar. Ivey and Bayleigh were very close.

When I was in Kokomo, Indiana, I started interviewing Ivey's crowd who had traveled to see his title fight the day before the match. I got more information from Ramona's parents than any other interview I have done. It was so broad a discussion that I could never put everything in the book, but I felt that the Chandlers knew Ivey better than he knew himself!

I took producer Chance "Rich" Richardson with me to video the interview with the Chandlers. Chance was gathering footage for a potential documentary about Johnathan Ivey's life and career. I was thankful we got this interview on film for that!

The Chandlers were Ivey's kind of people—loyal, trustworthy, and brutally honest communicators, laughing as they go. They told me of how early on Ivey attempted too hard to make a good impression. He used his fighting career to do so, and at one point said, "I am kind of a big deal." Unimpressed, Mrs. Chandler replied, "Yeah, I am kind of a big deal too." The couple broke out laughing as they told the story, and me and Chance soon joined them. Seeing an older woman who could crush the Monster was very amusing.

I hope producer Chance Rich includes much of our video interview with the Chandlers in Ivey's documentary, because that footage is worthy, and the viewers would find them funny, informative, and heart touching. Chance and I both felt enlightened to a new level on who Ivey was.

Ivey once informed me that he likes a solid female who is not afraid to step up in the home but doesn't run over the man in public. It sounded like he was describing Mrs. Chandler. Ramona's mother, Michelle Chandler is a very likable but forward person, who is quick to speak but who treats her husband respectfully. The potential mother-in-law had gained Ivey's admiration, and Ivey had won hers as well. One thing is sure: he always knew right where he stood with the Chandlers, and Ivey is the kind of guy who values that.

Since Ivey will not allow his daughter to get close to his girlfriends unless he feels she is a potential wife, he held Savannah back from meeting them at first. Mrs. Chandler confronted Ivey, telling him if he can't bring Savannah to meet them, then he needn't bother coming back over. Since he was serious about Ramona, he started taking Savannah to their home, and everyone liked one another.

The Chandlers told me they were impressed with both Ivey as a dad and Savannah as a daughter. He had also proved his fathering skills to them by treating Ramona's son like his own.

As I interviewed them, I mentioned Ivey saying the breakup was a huge mistake. They didn't blame Ivey; they said it was as much their hardheaded daughter as it was him. They attributed the breakup to Ivey being an emotional person and their daughter being stubborn. One interesting fact the Chandlers pointed out was that their daughter has not considered getting back with Ivey, but she also has never had another boyfriend since.

There was a touching moment in the interview with the Chandlers. The couple told of how great Ivey was with Ramona's son. They explained that Ivey was like a real dad to him. As they gave examples and details, they quoted the little boy's title he gave Ivey, "The Johnathan who loves me." Both the happy couple paused briefly to catch their breath, and they looked sad for a moment. It was one of those times where everyone in the room felt the emotion, and no one wanted to comment. I would call it, a moment of self-explanatory sorrow.

Ivey has been discouraged by his romances, but he has not given up. He believes the right one is still out there, and he is still trying to find her. Like every other angle of his life, his romantic life is volatile, but he is tough and will push on as he always does.

Romance has been perplexing for the Leg Lock Monster.

The Chandler family, whom Ivey loved enough to get all their names tattooed on him. Front left: Michelle, Ramona, Michael, and Bayleigh. Back: Robert.

CHAPTER 10

# First Impressions

> And when Saul had come to Jerusalem, he tried to
> join the disciples; but they were all afraid of him,
> and did not believe that he was a disciple.
> Acts 9:26 (NKJV)

"Don't judge a book by its cover." We have all heard it many times, but most of us keep right on doing it. This well-known phrase was one of the most common responses I heard when interviewing Ivey's crowd. No one could ever guess this guy would be so humble, honorable, kindhearted—the list goes on. The bottom line is that Ivey's appearance misleads people.

After I watched a video of Ivey preaching a sermon, I must admit it seemed odd, the monster preaching, but he did great. I thought back to a picture I saw on the Internet in which Jason the hockey mask–wearing serial slasher from the *Friday the 13th* films was up in front of a church crowd witnessing. The comical photo was used to make a point. We all stereotype by appearances. Too often this creates an atmosphere of unacceptance and makes progress hard for people.

Ivey had been baptized at the McKenzie Church of Christ when he was living near me. They had seen his progress, and even placed him chaperoning youth on the church's trip to a CYC event in Gatlinburg, Tennessee. He had the acceptance as a Christian he needed there.

Moving caused many problems in his youth, and his adulthood would be no exception. When he relocated to the Nashville area, he was not well received in church. Often after he arrived, sermons would start focusing on tattoos or other things that rejected or targeted him. It was as though he heard *You don't belong here; you will never fit in, so please leave.* Ivey has been discouraged with the church at times.

After twenty years of being a minister, I wish I could deny such things happen in churches, but I cannot. I've often witnessed social pressures misused to either run people out or hammer them into submission so that control freaks, hypocrites, and gossips could dominate the congregation. I gave up on my work at two churches for similar causes. Abuse and domination of the humble is the primary complaint I had about pulpit ministry. I prefer to teach now and just do guest speaking. My only plea is for people not to blame God for the sins of hypocritical churchgoing people, and I am glad to say Ivey does not.

Meeting Ivey is an experience for anyone. Some love him, some hate him, and some are terrified of him, but everyone has an intense reaction to him. Ivey has what I call an intense impression personality. You don't meet him and forget him because he leaves an impression, one way or another.

One night, Ivey and I ate at Cracker Barrel in Dickson. As we were leaving, I saw behind us was an older woman walking with a cane. I held the inner door to the foyer open for her, and she smiled and thanked me. Ivey opened the outer door for her. She hobbled very quickly past him and tried not to make eye contact.

We looked at each other, and he said, "You got a thank-you, I got a look like *Please don't kill me!*" Though we both laughed, I could tell it bothered him.

I agreed he had been judged wrongfully without a cause, but then pointed out that all the time, starry-eyed waitresses flirted with him, not me, and gave him free drinks or food, but not me. He could not deny this. We both realized the intensity of the impressions he has on people. Some admire his powerful image and his presence and are attracted to it and others are intimidated, but all have a response. That's what celebrity is all about, standing out in the crowd. He does it well.

## JOHNATHAN IVEY: THE MAN BEHIND THE MONSTER

It is not just little old ladies that find Ivey intimidating. In fact, when I interviewed former world kickboxing champion Anthony Maness, he volunteered his first impression of Ivey right away. They met at a small MMA show held in a bar. Ivey was the referee, and Anthony was the ISKA rep. Anthony admits to being shocked that anyone could be so intimidating in appearance yet be such a nice guy once you met him. Anthony spoke of it being such a clash of appearance versus persona.

From my first impression of Ivey on, I have observed everyone's first reaction to him. For this reason, one question I ask in every interview I conduct for this biography is, "What was your first impression of Johnathan Ivey?"

A notable pattern has resulted.

The most frequent observations made by those who meet Ivey are the many tattoos, gold teeth, muscles, and the absence of a neck. All these give him an intimidating appearance, Most all find Ivey to be much more humble and kind than his outwardness would indicate. Many have told me they were surprised by his faith in God. He is a man of conviction, despite being a bit rough around the edges, and people always notice this clash of expectations with factuality.

UFC fighter Dirty Harry Moskowitz told me he first saw Ivey right before their fight. He was expecting him to be very strong, and he was. Harry did not anticipate for Ivey to be so quick and was surprised by his speed. After they fought, they got to be friends, and Harry speaks very well of him, noting his humility and great personality.

One night at Harris Holt's MMA, when Ivey was doing a seminar, we arranged a list of interviews. I looked over the list of friends and fighters and noticed on the list was Ivey's barber. I was first shocked that a man who shaves his head goes to the barber, and secondly, shocked that he would be on the list of interviews. But there he was, Michael Weems.

I got to admit, I did not expect much from a barber. But he was the best interview that night. He was a real character, charming, knowledgeable, and funny. He said the first time Ivey walked into his shop, he saw his tattoos and gold teeth and was left with the impression *This is a crazy white guy.* That is the typical first conclusion from the African American crowd, but the two became great friends once they knew each other.

The barber told me of how much is hidden by Ivey's exterior. He spoke of Ivey's extreme humility as his most outstanding quality. Weems referred to Ivey as a gentle giant. As many others have said, you can't judge a book by its cover. He also mentioned Ivey as having an excellent father-daughter relationship with Savannah. Such qualities would be unexpected, judging by appearance.

When Ramona brought Ivey home as a date, the Chandlers responded with caution. Mrs. Chandler said her first impression was, *He is going to take my daughter.* She worried that he would surely impress her daughter and take her away. Robert explained his reaction: their oldest daughter, Ramona, had a crush on Ivey and wanted to date him. Mr. Chandler told the story of how he pulled Ivey off to the side to ask him, "You're not going to kidnap my daughter, are you?"

When he explained his protective feelings, he said, "She wanted to go out with him, and if you know what Johnathan looks like, I mean, I am not the cleanest guy—" His statement was interrupted, first by him laughing, then by all the rest of us as well. In a lot of ways, the first impression shock factor of his appearance opens the door to people being pleasantly surprised if they will take the time to know him. Many never give him a chance.

Looking back at the many times Ivey and I hung out and ate together, I call to mind my favorite quote from him. We had often joked about him looking like the guy a mobster sends to collect money. He was talking about staying out of trouble at the time and said, "Do you have any idea how easy I am to pick out of a police lineup?" Everyone at our table laughed loudly, calling attention to ourselves. I often wonder what the people eating around us thought when overhearing our conversations.

I'm trying to recall anyone who didn't change their mind about Ivey after getting to know him, and I can name only one: Fred Dulay, Ivey's boxing coach. He had recognized both sides of Ivey from the start. I credit this to not only his intelligence but also to his experience. As a boxing coach, he knows fighters well. Fighters tend to have all these well-hidden insecurities and flaws, and he knows this.

My all-time favorite of the first impressions of Ivey would have to be that of Jeremy "the Gravedigger" Wallace. The pro MMA fighter was a stand-up stylist with real knockout power despite his small size. I had a chance meeting with Jeremy at a charity fundraiser called the Amazing Race. Years ago, I trained with Jeremy, and we grappled often; but I was not crazy enough to box him. As we were catching up, I mentioned Ivey's biography. Unsolicited, he told me the story of the day he met the Monster.

Early in his life, he was trying to gain some more ground-fighting experience, so he traveled to Kentucky and entered a grappling tournament. He won the lightweight division at only one hundred and twenty pounds.

Next, there was a grand championship. If he could defeat the heavyweight champion, he could take home the overall prize. The inspired teen gladly agreed to the challenge, having no idea who had won the heavyweight championship until he looked across the mat and saw Johnathan Ivey for the first time. His heart sank, and he thought, *They are crazy!* For pride reasons, he would not back out.

Johnathan was way more than twice his size and could have hurt the teen Gravedigger quickly, but instead, he pressed him over his head and walked around with him. Ivey entertained the crowd by gently clowning with his small opponent before cautiously defeating him. Jeremy Wallace esteems Ivey highly to this day over that first impression.

It is hard to hide a monster, even when he is well dressed! First impressions of Ivey often throw people, until they get to know him. Ivey here is the best man at his closest friend Sam Taylor's wedding.

There is just something about Ivey's appearance that people take wrong.

CHAPTER 11

# The Stress of Johnathan Ivey's First Show

> Knowing that the testing of your faith produces patience.
> —James 1:3 (NKJV)

When Ivey first told me he was getting into promoting, I warned him about the stress involved. I explained the most stressful day of my entire life was the day of the first MMA show I ever promoted. I knew it would be hard for him, but just like fighting, I had complete confidence he was going to do what he had to and do it well.

Ivey had cut a deal with a financial supporter to make the show happen. The handshake agreement was done to supply the needed upfront cash in return for a cut of the show's income. He had already done this before talking to me, or I would have gladly backed the show's frugal budget. As it turned out, this deal was unnecessary because advance ticket sales for seats and private tables funded the show entirely, Ivey never accessed the upfront money, but he did keep his word on the investor's cut.

The first wave of stress is arranging the venue and date. Trying to find the right location available on a required day and at an economical price can take days, or even weeks, of phone calls. Venues in the Nashville area seem much higher than in many other parts of Tennessee. Ivey settled on a large building located on the fairgrounds in Nashville, which had a building available that would be large enough at a reasonable price. The problem seemed to be solved—that is, until the weekend of the show when all that went very bad.

Next, Ivey needed the sanctioning body that oversees the show; he was pleased that ISKA rep Anthony Maness was available for the date. Maness, a former world kickboxing champion with a legendary undefeated record, was as knowledgeable and as trustworthy as they come. The well-respected Maness had served as a judge for some UFC events and was an excellent choice for walking Ivey through the legalistic end of his new promotion.

As expected, the fight card had a few common problems. Some fighters were hard to match with their size and experience levels. Some pulled out of the card for various reasons. Ivey had fewer difficulties with this than most more experienced promoters commonly encounter. I attribute fighters' respect for Ivey to this going as smoothly as it did, along with his friendship with coaches. He had some points of anxiety working on the card, but I was assured he was getting off easy and it would turn out fine. The final result was one match fell through. Otherwise, all went well.

We often spoke as the card drew closer, and he was haunted by two fears—losing money and looking bad. His famous name was his most significant asset, but that name also raised expectations of the quality this event would offer. Being a legendary fighter does not make someone an expert promoter. Fortunately, Ivey's supporters did not believe that, and their confidence was enabling him to be both.

Fox was a Marine Corps–trained mechanic and nitpicking when it came to being organized. When he had helped me with shows in the past, he had a checklist of all the little things promoters often forget. I sent the list to Ivey's phone. Minutes later, I got the reply thanking me, but saying he had not thought of anything on that long list.

On that list was MMA gloves, which must be approved by the ISKA. I offered my gloves. Before the show, I discovered my gloves stolen. In a panic, I found attractive gloves on clearance cheaper than I would have imagined, and rush-ordered them. Once again, we survived another challenge.

There are countless things to arrange for these events. The paramedic team, ambulance service, ringside physician, ring girls, judges, timekeeper, referees, and cage rental, just to name a few. I had given him the facts; one man cannot do it alone. He accepted this, and I took on the task of arranging officials and assigning the seating around the cage, as well as gathering all the needed supplies for the event. Fox and others were right there helping out every inch of the way. He also enlisted Latisha Walden a former promoter and current trusted friend. Latisha helped with permits, payments, insurance, and other legwork. I was very thankful for her, as she took care of all the things I hate doing. Ivey was overwhelmingly busy, but still had enough help to allow him time to focus on the card.

I have never seen a first show come together that well for any rookie promoter. With the fights growing close, all looked well. I could not click on Facebook without being covered up with match outcome predictions and other hype for the show. Ivey was still stressed. I laughed that he was having anxiety about a show that was selling out of private tables and already fully funded by advance sales! It was already a success before it happened, but still, I knew what he was going through all too well.

My first show, I received over four hundred text messages and more than one hundred calls on the day of the show. I knew the stress would cover him like a wave, so I encouraged him to brace himself. I explained that the shows are always hard, but that they would eventually turn out fine in the end.

On top of all these and, other anxieties appeared an enormous unforeseen blow. The Faire Grounds had double-booked the venue! You can get by without certain things, but a location is not one of them. On the weekend of the show, Ivey came to set up the building, only to find out there was a dog show there. They apologized and offered another building, which was not big enough but was the only alternative. At this point, Ivey was in a full panic, thinking things could not be worse. But they could, and did, get worse.

We had set up the building as well as we could Friday evening, accepting the fact we would lose a few hundred seats. However, that night, someone called the fire marshal to report the event as hazardous for evacuation in the unlikely event of a fire. This pathetic act was most likely sabotage from another promotion who misused the law to harm Ivey's attempt to be a promoter. The results were that the fire marshal removed more than two hundred more seats and some prepaid private tables. Ivey was devastated!

On the day of the show, I could not get off work at the post office due to a shortage of employees. Fox who was a judge and helping out with many things is employed there as well. We had told Ivey the moment we got off work we would come. We gave him an approximate arrival time of two hours before the show.

Fox and I raced around our mail routes and were off about an hour early. Having the smaller route, I took a portion of Fox's route to speed us up. We thought all was well, unaware yet of the sabotage.

I had barely made it home when I got a message from Ivey. He said that everything was falling apart, he could not do this. The text said he was leaving and going to the movies, the card was mine. I could run it, and he would pay me. I messaged Fox and said we have to leave for Nashville immediately. I recalled my first event; I too started to walk out from the overwhelming stress. I messaged Ivey and said I would handle everything, and that if anyone needed anything, to send them to me. "But stay there!"

As Fox and I raced to Nashville, which is about an hour and twenty minutes from my home, I told him, "I have no clue how I can stop Ivey, but he is not leaving!" He was so close to fulfilling his goal. I could not bear the thought of him folding now. I was counting on the fact that Ivey would not hit me in front of his friends and family because he would look bad.

Later, I found out that Latisha was also stopping him from leaving on that end as I raced there. No one could stop Ivey physically, so we all had to gang up on him from every other aspect possible. The final saving grace was a total stranger who was a minister. He spotted Ivey in his anxiety and walked up to him and said, "God told me to come talk to you." Ivey became overwhelmed with emotion. The man counseled Ivey, calming his nerves; and shortly after, Fox and I arrived. I told Ivey to walk around, greet people, and look confident, it was all going to work out. Latisha, Fox, and I tried to handle as many of the distractions as possible to keep Ivey's stress load as light as possible.

One thing I remember from my promoting days is how often you need extra seating. I had hidden several folding chairs under the cage just in case, and they came in handy being overlooked by the fire marshal. I wish I had stashed away several hundred. Ivey was forced to refund money for prepaid seating and sell the standing room at a lower price. Though discouraging, it was a smart call on his part, and standing room allows way more people per square foot than furniture does.

Ticket lines wrapped around the fair grounds, and the building filled to the point where no more could enter. It was bittersweet; the great success of the show was celebrating in the shadow of the potential success that could have been even greater.

ISKA rep Anthony Maness and I tried to encourage Ivey, explaining that these things happen. We reassured him it was the best first show turnout any promoter we knew had ever achieved. Ivey seemed calmer and was hiding his anxiety well, but he was struggling.

Despite his struggling emotions and anxiety, when the lights dimmed, and the music started, Ivey transformed into precisely the celebrity promoter his supporters expected and paid to see. No one in the crowd could see anything except the cage hero they all loved putting on his first show. Blessed as always, Ivey survived everything that came at him, just as he still does.

At a much later date, I interviewed Anthony Maness. He spoke of how impressed with Ivey's show he was that night. Anthony has levels of experience beyond imagination; his reaction was total confidence in Ivey's ability as a promoter. Anthony said Ivey has the charisma that won him a great following. That quality, combined with a natural talent for putting together a quality show, made him the best first-time promoter he had ever seen.

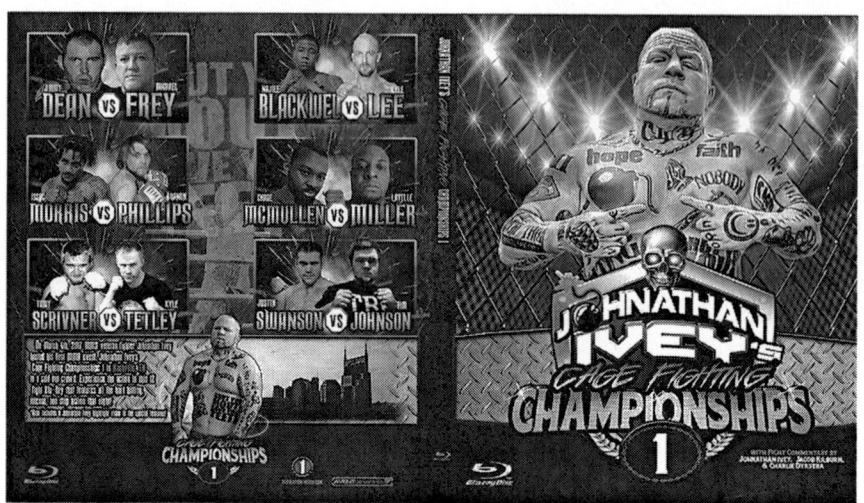

Johnathan Ivey's *Cage Fighting Champions* sold out on the very first show, despite his struggles!

CHAPTER 12

# The Monster's Return to the Cage

> Be anxious for nothing, but in everything
> by prayer and supplication,
> with thanksgiving, let your requests be made known to God;
> and the peace of God, which surpasses all understanding,
> will guard your hearts and minds through Christ Jesus.
> —Philippians 4:6–7 (NKJV)

After being knocked out in Japan, Ivey had taken a break from fighting, and that is why he had started promoting. He needed income. With his first promoting success, he now had the means to pay bills temporarily, but not indefinitely. He still needed to consider both a second event or fighting again.

It was difficult to say which was harder, considering putting himself through the overwhelming stress of promoting again or climbing back into the cage after a disheartening knockout in Japan at age forty-one. He chose to do both. Ivey is the type to face both his fears at the same time, and that is what he did. He started planning the next show and opened his mind to his comeback fight. Returning to the cage would be a reasonable time to consider a less challenging matchup on an undercard to safely ease back into the game. However, Johnathan Ivey is not known for being either reasonable or safe.

He was offered a title fight for the vacant Colosseum Combat Heavy Weight Championship in Kokomo, Indiana. He accepted it, of course. But he repeatedly told me that if he lost, it would be his last fight.

The promoter of Colosseum Combat was Mark Slater. Ivey highly esteemed Mark, which helped him with the decision to return to the cage. Myself, I did not like the fact that the opponent was from Kokomo. On this occasion, Ivey was the more trusting one of the two of us. I had encountered some biased refs and judges in my time when it came to the hometown favorites, but Ivey had no worries at all. With Mark Slater being the promoter, Ivey had confidence everything would be fair and honest.

When I sent Mr. Slater a request for an interview, I received a very polite response almost immediately. I was impressed right away with how down to earth and friendly he was. Mostly, I wanted to ask how he decided on Ivey for the title fight.

He explained the significance of this show. It fell on his dad's seventy-fifth birthday, and he wanted to put on a memorable night in his honor. He had followed Ivey for years and admired him as an MMA legend, and as a father as well. Mark said that he had enjoyed the father-daughter videos of Ivey and Savanah that were online, which, he said, "melted my heart." He was impressed with Ivey's values and could not think of a better human being to represent his promotion if he won the title.

I was impressed with Mark as a person and a promoter right away. I understood Ivey trusting him. Mark saw past the cage and admired the man behind the monster, but he had not by any means lost sight of business. Ivey is known for his big entrances and would put on a memorable show for the fans. He called Ivey one of the most entertaining fighters he has ever seen.

Since I represented Ivey, we discussed only him, and neither of us ever mentioned the opponent at all. But what if Ivey were to lose? Any promoter would consider either possibility, what if either man were champion? I had too much respect for Mark to ask that awkward question, but I had already noted the intelligence of his matchmaking. Ivey was fighting a hometown hero. One way, the promotion gets a legendary champ like Ivey, and the other way, they get a hometown hero who will draw a crowd as champion. It was a win-win situation and smart promoting.

## JOHNATHAN IVEY: THE MAN BEHIND THE MONSTER

Ivey started the training but missed some days due to illness. His confidence levels seemed to vary from day to day. I was confident in his abilities but concerned with where he stood emotionally relating to his return to the cage. My experience as a counselor was haunting me at this point. When Ivey got knocked out in Japan, he healed physically; but his self-esteem was severely damaged. I had counseled far too many people with their abilities crippled by low self-esteem.

I soon noticed patterns: when we discussed the ground, he would say things like, "I am going to break his leg." I had no doubt he could, and I was encouraged by his confidence. That was the old Johnathan Ivey with the reputation for being the monster.

There was another pattern that did not encourage me. When we talked concerning the possibility of going to the later rounds, or even the decision, his confidence level fell fast. He seemed concerned about getting knocked out, something he rarely worried about before his fight in Japan. The Japan trip was a bad experience in many ways and had taken its toll on Ivey.

Due to the international location, he was accompanied by Lance Boyd; but he was unable to have his usual support group with him, which always hurts his performance in the cage. Ivey was also treated poorly by the Japanese promotion. Ivey's emotional weaknesses got exploited in Japan, and he took damage that had not healed.

While in Japan, they met an interpreter. she was a waitress who had volunteered her time to escort him and Lance around and translated for them. But when Ivey requested that the interpreter be allowed to come with him to the show, the promotion coldly refused his request. He was embarrassed to have to disallow the kind woman from attending and was angry over the insulting absence of hospitality. Nonetheless, he was a professional and delivered well.

He had been instructed to present himself as the bad guy since he was foreign. They may have gotten more than they bargained for, as Ivey was now angry. He did his *Karate Kid*-style crane kick stance to mock the Japanese culture, as well as other offenses. But most of all, he staged various disruptions to cause problems, pretending to be unaware due to the language barrier. After all, they denied him his

English-speaking companion to translate, and he intended to make them regret that insulting dishonor.

Frustration and lack of emotional support, however, was not what cost him the fight in the end. He was knocked out by a punch that would not have fazed him just a few years ago. Far worse than the physical damage was the blow to his confidence.

Ivey explained to me that each time you come out of the cage, you are a little less of the man you were when you went in. He is right. The body can only absorb so much damage, but his greatest danger was the confidence he lost. He now believed he could be suddenly knocked out, and that hurt more than punches.

I honestly believe most of us who were close to Ivey were not that worried about him getting hurt in the upcoming title fight. However, we all had our concerns about his emotional well-being. He was struggling with an inner conflict. His toughest opponent was himself, and that was who I feared might beat him.

The next concern I had was that if Ivey lost, could he live with going out on that loss? Could he look back at his career and be satisfied with all his past glory and accept the adverse outcomes of the last few fights? I got past this when I admitted the answer was likely a no. He could not end his career that way. This adventure was more than a fight; it may as well been a duel with this much on the line!

## JOHNATHAN IVEY: THE MAN BEHIND THE MONSTER

Ivey with one of his many opponents that he defeated in the first round.

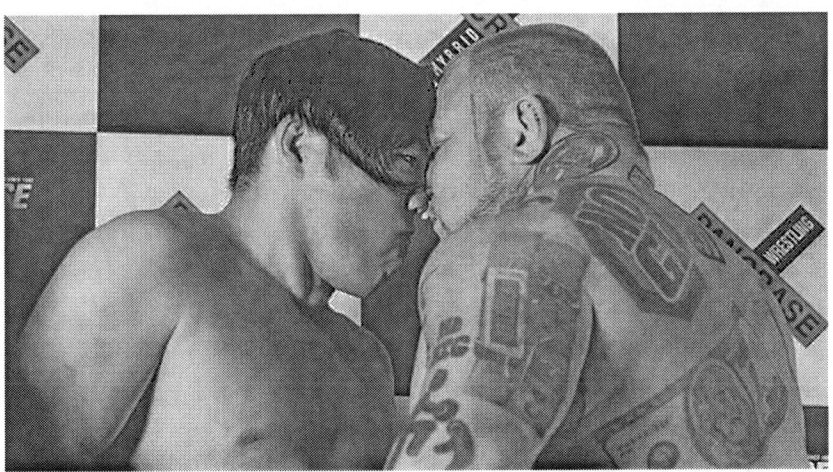

Ivey in Japan, before getting knocked out by a punch that would not have hurt him just a few years ago. Was it time to retire? The upcoming title shot would answer that question!

CHAPTER 13

# The Monster at the Crossroads

> Let us, therefore, come boldly to the throne of grace,
> that we may obtain mercy and find grace to help in time of need.
> —Hebrews 4:16 (NKJV)

The years come and go fast. As time pressed on, Ivey found himself middle-aged, a place fighters do not want to be. Money was tight, injuries stayed longer, and the future looked uncertain. Ivey knew he was not prepared for things as fast as they were coming.

He had reached the crossroads of his career. He was both putting together his second show and preparing for what could be his final fight (if he were to lose) at the same time! He was doing both for the same reason: he needs the money to take care of his child. As usual, he had to go with the flow of opportunities.

The fight held much significance. It was not only a title fight, it had numerable other pressures. The opponent was pretty much a pure striker, and Ivey is pretty much a pure grappler. It would be simple; this man had no chance against Ivey's skills on the ground. However, Ivey had little chance of winning on his feet. It would be a classic battle of striker versus grappler to make the other man fight their fight.

Ivey's opponent would have the advantage of fighting in his hometown. The crowd would be cheering for him, and for Ivey, that is a huge psychological disadvantage. You could contribute most of his losses to one of two things—either short notice with little or no time to prepare, or he had little or no emotional support from friends and supporters. Supporters are such a great need for him that he typically in the past had chosen friends over trainers for his cornermen, often picking someone who knows nothing about the sport at all but who encouraged him.

For this fight, he asked me to travel to Indiana and be a corner for him, which I was honored to do. I do know the sport; but more importantly for him, I am a trusted friend. He would have at least that much advantage. Though I wish I had more to offer him, I reminded myself he once had a corner man who drank the water he was supposed to bring Ivey at the end of the round.

There was not a lot of insight I could give him, but I looked up what I could about his opponent. I liked what I saw. He had little experience against grapplers; he seemed to target fights with strikers. Since Ivey can grapple with the best of the best, this gave me a boost in confidence.

The opponent also struggled with finishing, so knocking Ivey out was unlikely. Still, the fact remained that Ivey had ended 98 percent of his wins in the first round. The psychological effect of hearing the bell at the end of the first round would be devastating. He would likely lose a decision if he didn't win quickly and would win fast if he gets the opponent to the ground. I had never seen a fight more dependent on a single takedown for the outcome.

Another disadvantage Ivey faced was the divided mind. It is hard to worry about two things at once. He was at the crossroads on both his primary sources of income. That is a lot to have to spin around in the mind of an emotional person. Still, I have seen Ivey at his best and worst. I knew he would be stressed and nervous, but I also knew that when the lights dimmed and the music started, it was his world, and the monster would come out.

If I were an oddsmaker, my honest evaluation with no bias would have to be five to one in Ivey's favor; in fact, I bet one hundred dollars on this fight. I am not a gambler. I made the mistake of helping build up the event online by doing some hype talk and was called out by Ivey's opponent publicly to bet him one hundred dollars. So I had no choice but to accept.

The challenger Ivey faced had only a tenth of his experience, and even less than a tenth of his talent on the ground. Though Ivey faced a superior striker, mixed martial arts has proven many times that it is harder for a striker to make a grappler stand up than for a grappler to make a striker go down. Experience has taught me not to bet on the striker. They win some, but not most.

Similarly, I was betting on his show as a success as well. First and foremost, he just has so many supporters that the coverage reached so many potential ticket buyers. On top of this potential, I had watched this card come together, and it was going to be a classic. The match-ups were incredible. On an average MMA card, there are a few key matchups everyone is paying to see, and the rest is just to fill the card out. With this card, every bout was at least good, and most were intensely exciting.

As of one month out, Ivey had sold eleven of the twenty-five private tables. The early sales were encouraging because the higher prices on a private table and reserved seats are what pay the expenses on the show, so if Ivey could sell all those, he at least knew he would not lose money and would begin to show a profit. Most private table customers start buying about two weeks before the show, so this looked favorable, but not enough to calm Ivey's nerves.

When we discussed the stress he was under, he broke it down rather simply. Other than the financial worries, his fear of both the show and the fight was embarrassing himself, and he could potentially do that at either. I understood his concerns but was confident he was creating a vaster potential failure than what was at all likely.

Fortunately, in the week that followed, several more private tables sold and took much of the pressure off. It became apparent that all the tables would be sold out, and that would indicate significant ticket sales as well. My prediction was that Ivey would make enough to carry him throughout the remainder of the year and win the heavyweight championship as well.

When we discussed the biography and the fact that he was at the crossroads, I said the ending was about to write itself. Ivey replied that he hoped he could give a happy ending to the book. He said he could win the belt and sell out the show. He might do one or the other, or maybe he would get knocked out, and no one would show up for the show, and then the book can end with him killing himself. (And we both laughed.)

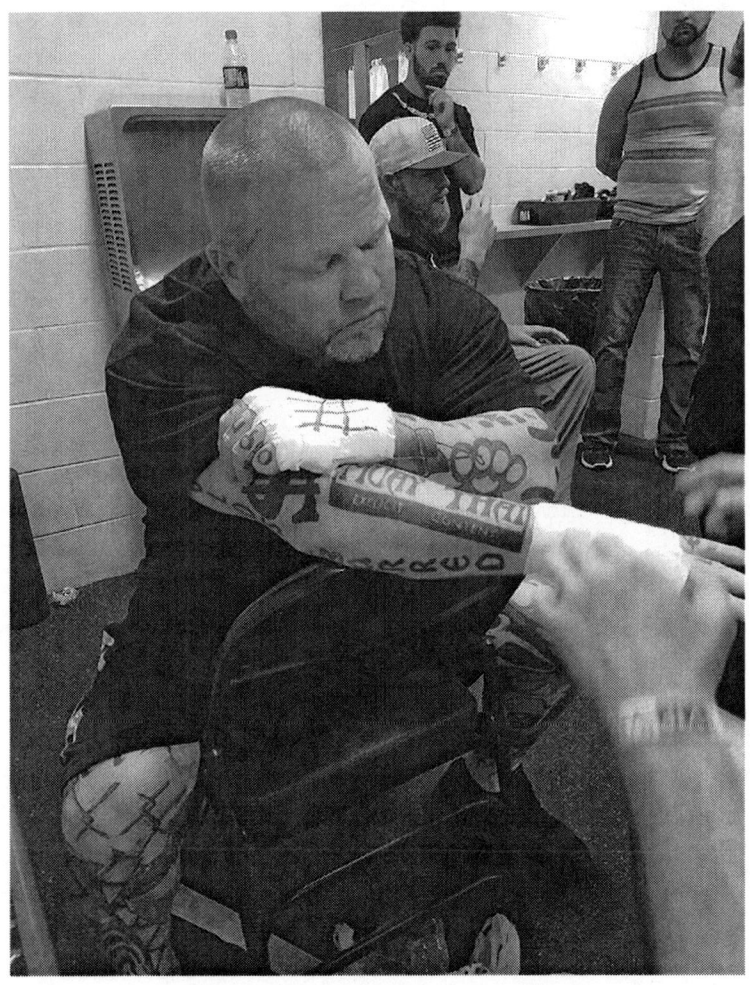

Facing the crossroads of his life: could this be
the end or just a new beginning?

CHAPTER 14

# The Light at the End of the Tunnel of Stress

If God is for us, who can be against us?
—Romans 8:31 (NKJV)

Ivey's first show was very hard for him. He had survived all the unforeseen happenings, such as venue change, fire marshal removing two hundred chairs and some private tables, as well as the various other stress factors. In the MMA business, we all learn as we go, and Ivey was looking forward to doing better this time.

After the Nashville Fair Grounds had double-booked the building last time, causing a chain-reaction disaster, he could never bring himself to trust them again. Ivey rarely gives a second chance after being done wrong. He hates to deal with anyone whom he struggles to believe, which supplies him a short list of allies.

The first goal was a better venue with a target of seating at least eight hundred people. Finding a place that size in Nashville was comfortable, finding one that did not charge more than ticket sales could generate proved hard. I called about one often used for large weddings, and it was eight thousand a night with no chairs. In time, Ivey abandoned the search and decided to try neighboring cities. After weeks of searching, he booked the Murfreesboro Expo Center with great worries that supporters may not drive an extra thirty minutes from Nashville. It still was over his budget and did not come with tables and chairs. The more expensive venue, plus renting the furnishings, began to make this show a very high-stakes risk, adding thousands of dollars to the budget.

Few fighters have thousands in cash available, and Ivey was no exception. Anyone who thinks I say Ivey is an honorable man just because I am writing a book about him should be silenced by what happened next. I withdrew eight thousand dollars in cash from my bank account and handed it to him with no worries at all. We had nothing in writing, just a pile of money from my hand to his. I saw in his first event that he has what it takes to be a success, and his character is such that I would never worry about him stealing my money. I put my money where my mouth is because I believed in Ivey more than he believes in himself.

He was more nervous than I was, and I was the one who put up the money for the show. However, the worries ran farther than just those extra expenses. Next came the permits required for concessions and beverage sales that were different in Murfreesboro. Fees to apply and time requirements soon revealed that it would be just about impossible to have profitable concessions at this show. Still, I believed Ivey could balance the budget with ticket sales and come out well.

Next came the emotional level of stress. In the first show, ISKA rep Anthony Maness had helped Ivey hold up under pressure with the reassurance that all the problems were quite well-known to these events and can be dealt with as they come. Anthony is a rare type of man; he is a former kickboxing world champion with a legendary record, yet had no big ego and was a kindhearted person who loves to help and encourage others. Anthony makes the short list of people whom Ivey trusts and was a lifesaver at that show. In light of this, Ivey had messaged Anthony to make sure he was available to be the ISKA rep who oversaw his second effort. The thought of having someone to answer to other than Anthony was unspeakable. Unfortunately, the unforeseen happened: the Bellator promotion chose the same night, August 19, for a show in East Tennessee. The ISKA, of course, responded by moving their head man in the state, Anthony Maness, to that larger show.

When I read about Anthony being over at the Bellator show, I messaged him with my concerns that Ivey would be stressed out about a sub. He assured me it would be a worthy one, which I didn't doubt, but I questioned whether it was one that Ivey would find comfortable. I explained Anthony was a security blanket to Ivey on his stress at the last show and reminded him of Ivey's anxiety. In a judgment call, I decided it was better to break the bad news to Ivey before allowing the show to get closer, when he would be under more pressure. I messaged him to explain, and I received a reply saying he could not discuss it yet, or he would say things he would regret. I knew this was not going to go well.

Later in the evening, he messaged me back. It would be an understatement to say he was upset. He had had some differences before with the sub that was suggested and did not want him at his show. I messaged Anthony Maness and requested Jason Wood. Wood had been a rep for many years, and Ivey trusted him, but he had now retired from it. Jason and Ivey had sparred some and liked each other. Anthony said he would check if Jason would return to do one more event. I told Ivey, "Now we pray Jason Wood agrees and wait."

The prayer was answered, and as usual, God had a better idea.

The next day, I received a message from Anthony Maness that said bluntly, "Can you call me." His cell number was attached. I had known and admired Anthony ten years, and never once did he ask me to call him. I said out loud, "Uh-oh, this can't be good!" My gut instinct said Ivey had called him and exploded.

I quickly called Anthony, and he said, "Listen, Ivey has flipped his wig." Describing Ivey's temper, he said, "I consider Johnathan to be one of my best friends, and I had no idea he was like that."

I replied with a joking tone, "Oh yeah, he is very like that." I was relieved to hear Anthony laughing. I started laughing too, and the conversation went well from there.

Anthony then said he had a solution and didn't know why he had not thought of it before. He mentioned that I had been involved in so many MMA shows and worked with the ISKA so many times as an official that I was qualified to be an ISKA rep, so he was approving me as one, and I would be the rep at Ivey's show. I was as silent as if Anthony had landed one of his famous kicks into my stomach. I had wanted to be an ISKA rep for ten years, but never even tried. I knew two reps personally, Anthony and Jason Wood: one was a legendary world champion and one never lost a fight until he fought for a world title. I was speechless! God had answered our prayers beyond our expectation.

Anthony had first talked to Ivey about his decision and asked him if he trusted me. Ivey had replied that he would walk through broken glass for me. So Anthony gave his judgment, and the problem was solved. Everyone got a happy ending, especially me!

Ivey managed to find some vendors who had a license that met the approval of the strict local requirements on concessions. They negotiated for Ivey to receive a small flat fee. It was nothing to brag about, but it brought quality food to the show and added a bit of income for Ivey. It was a solution to a stressful problem, and at this point, Ivey needed that more than the money.

I quickly found a replacement for myself as timekeeper since there was no way to do both jobs. Tony Muller was a well-respected judo instructor in Tennessee who had been through ISKA training, and he was glad to fill in my spot. The next few days, we were far from stress-free, but we all felt much better about the upcoming show. There was light at the end of the tunnel.

ISKA rep and former world kickboxing champ Anthony Maness.

## CHAPTER 15

# Road Trip to Kokomo

> A man who has friends must himself be friendly,
> but there is a friend who sticks closer than a brother.
> —Proverbs 18:24 (NKJV)

I arrived in Kokomo, Indiana, and got settled and immediately started observing the team Ivey had assembled for the trip for his championship match on the Coliseum Combat card. He had some of his inner circle in his room with us, and more who traveled to meet him there for his title fight.

That weekend was an emotional time for Ivey. He had not publicly announced his decision, that he would either win the title or accept the fact that it is time to retire. He wanted as many of his closest friends around him as possible for this emotional point in his life. He has always drawn strength from loyal friends, and the time he spends unwinding with them helps him prepare mentally and emotionally for the fight.

Staying in the same room with us, all of whom rode with him to the destination were three of his closest allies. All very different types of people. The odd crew meshed well for Ivey, and I blended in best I could. I was taking in the personality of each to help me better know what makes Ivey tick, for the biography. I was not disappointed by the effort. Early on, it was agreed that I would interview each one in our downtime, and we selected the mornings for interviews to avoid the busy day's schedule.

## JOHNATHAN IVEY: THE MAN BEHIND THE MONSTER

Being a morning person, I woke before the others and took my laptop to the hotel lobby for free coffee and breakfast. I was the first one there, as always. I began typing notes, and later, fighters from the card started coming in. I spoke to several, but one stood out—a very likable young black man with dreadlocks. We talked awhile, and later on, Jacob Kilburn informed me that it was UFC fighter Dominque Steele. I googled his picture, and sure enough, it was him. I did not recognize him because in his promo photos, he looks mean, but in person, he had a friendly manner about him. I later found out he was the main event on the next Colosseum Combat event but had traveled to this show, which preceded the one he would be on. I couldn't help but make the connection; once again, Ivey was fighting on the same level with UFC fighters, but remained overlooked.

After a few hours and way too many cups of coffee, Ivey's crew started waking up. The first was Chance "Rich" Richardson. If I had to choose the man that least fit into our odd group that weekend, he would probably be my choice just because he was the only nonfighter.

Chance was an up-and-coming film and audio producer who was working on Ivey's documentary and shooting everything in sight that could have value. He was the quietest of us all, but focused, intelligent, and driven. Chance was a good-natured family man with an innocent look, appearing to be in his late teens to his early twenties, but was actually over thirty. He grows a beard at his wife's request, because she was tired of people thinking he was her son!

This determined overachiever was juggling a full-time job, family commitments, and his production studio, which he had wisely built himself across the street from his home in a residential neighborhood. The building was designed to look like a simple storage building on the outside but well equipped inside where it counts. Located in Nashville, Chance's undercover studio was probably saving him six digits on location expenses, construction, and as a plus, it helped him avoid several permits and zoning rules. I admired his overachieving beating the system drive. He was my kind of guy, and we got along well.

Chance's relationship to Ivey was simple; he was a self-proclaimed "fan turned friend." A rare exception to Ivey's rule of keeping people at a distance. After getting to know Chance, it was not hard to see why Ivey let him in. He is the type a stranger can look at and trust; in a word, he is harmless and looks the part.

The next one down was Jacob Kilburn, by far the most complicated personality of the group—other than Ivey himself, that is. Jacob was an undefeated pro fighter with a style that blended karate and kickboxing with jiujitsu for the ground fighting. He was very fast and had the element of surprise because he looked thin and passive. Jacob earned his nickname the Killer in the cage with his split personality. He turned from an intellectual to stone cold when fighting.

Jacob was religious, the son of a preacher. He shared his views freely on both religion and conspiracy theories. Jacob is a firm believer that the earth is flat, and everyone from Christopher Columbus to NASA has suppressed the truth to support the lies of the round earth. When he explained this to me, I thought he was joking. I soon found out Jacob is not alone. This is a massive movement. After hearing him describe it and seeing the movement's materials and theories online, I went from thinking they were crazy to not caring what shape the earth is and having no interest in debating the topic. My money is still on round, but if God made it, I am good with whatever shape it is. I respected his convictions and avoided the topic from then on.

Jacob and I clashed in other areas as well. I chose not to comment on most of his views. Not only was I the newest member of Ivey's inner circle, but I hate debates in general. I feel that arguing is usually a waste of time and has little power to change anyone's opinion or beliefs.

Jacob and I had met before a few times. Both of us were color commentators doing a voice-over for Ivey's first fight card in Chance's studio. We never meshed well that night; it was an awkward introduction, and then suddenly we were working together.

Later, I took an invitation from Ivey to go to Clarksville to Harris Holt's gym when Ivey was doing a seminar. Fox and my fighter friend Chaz Jordan, a former light heavyweight champ, came with me. Chaz was told to find some kickboxing gear from the shelves, by random chance, he got Jacob's equipment instead of what belonged to the gym. Jacob got angry over the mistake. I did not like Jacob, and neither did Fox or Chaz.

I had often wondered how it was that Ivey, with his temper, never ended up killing Jacob. Ivey explained to me that even though Jacob was opinionated and outspoken, he was a great guy. He was just easy to take wrong. I had described what Ivey said to Chaz and Fox later on. I told them maybe Ivey was right, or maybe Ivey had been hit in the head too much. We all laughed it off, and the incident was forgotten.

I was prepared for the worst sharing a room with Jacob, fearing it would be nonstop verbal conflict, but Ivey was right. Jacob is a good guy. I realized that everything I did not like about Jacob was very minor, but his primary qualities were all good. Jacob is, under normal circumstances, quite respectful and humble. He is just easy to take wrong because he communicates his feelings more boldly than most, so he often does not make good first impressions.

Ivey and Ricky often reacted to Jacob's opinions with a sharp tone. The flare-ups were never confrontational. I would describe all their communication as sibling rivalry at the very worst times. Before the trip ended, I was honored to be part of the team I had bonded with and grown to understand. I thought of this group as one big happy but slightly dysfunctional family.

Since Jacob and I were getting along just fine, I could not resist pranking him a little. Ivey had previously expressed concern to me about how Jacob and I would get along on this trip. When Jacob and I both returned to the room together, Ivey asked how it went, I replied loud and clear, "It went well, but I had no idea that Jacob has tapped you out twenty-three times until he told me about it!" Jacob took less than a second to respond. "I didn't say that!" Except for Jacob, everyone found this amusing. All who know Ivey know he has a real issue with tapping out even in sparring. Ivey knew I was joking when I said this. I have pulled this prank before after interviews, but Jacob had no clue of that.

Ricky Ward slept through his interview, twice. That morning, he slept late, and we had to drive to Indianapolis from Kokomo and get back before weigh-ins, so we rescheduled. Later, when I arranged to interview him again, he took a nap and slept through it once more! I got to know him more through the group travels and dinners.

Ricky has a deep voice, was athletic, and in excellent shape, especially for his age. On the first impression, I would say he is the rugged type, similar to a confident middle-aged drill sergeant, but slightly quieter and more humble.

Ricky is more of a traditional martial artist than the rest of the team. He is Brazilian jiujitsu black belt, and in that sport, black belts don't come easy. Ricky works with Ivey on his ground game, though Ivey's style is far from Ricky's; Ivey incorporates in much of what Ricky teaches him.

Ricky and Ivey are close friends as well. Ricky used his gym for one of Ivey's challenge matches. The match was one of those many times someone bet on themselves as they challenged Ivey to a fight.

The usual routine is the challengers insult Ivey, frequently calling him overrated or unimpressive, and state online that they are better than him. Ivey accepts, but only if they bet on themselves. Ivey matches the bet, and of course, adds the critic's money to his household budget.

Ricky is no exception to the random personalities of Ivey's team. Ricky believes in traditional martial arts, which means wearing a uniform (called a Gi): colored belts to distinguish rank, and bowing to an opponent out of respect. The irony of Ricky's friendship with Ivey is Ivey says traditional martial arts equals poop!"

Somehow these two get along well together.

There was a small flare-up in the back of my SUV in our travels that weekend over the traditional belt ranking system. Ricky feels that Ivey needs to test for rank in the art of jiujitsu, knowing Ivey's abilities are high level. Jacob, who works for the Harris Holt Martial Arts Gym, which also offers MMA, agreed with Ricky. Ivey said he could not see any gain in being handed any belt unless it's gold.

Chance and I were in the front quietly listening to the war of words in the back. Finally, someone, I don't recall who, asked my opinion. I said Ivey should get tested for the belts so he would have something else to sell. Everyone laughed, and the debate ended on that note. I was just joking, but everyone who knows Ivey knows he sells all his belts and trophies. His traditional martial arts belts would meet the same fate if he had them.

When the five of us arrived in Indianapolis, we went on a bit of a scavenger hunt. The idea was to design Ivey the ultimate showstopping entrance. Ivey loves big intimidating entrances and loves horror; we wanted something related. The first stop was a costume shop. We settled on an orange prison jumpsuit like the one worn by Hannibal Lecter, and the same type of mask Lecter wore while strapped to the dolly for safe transporting in the movie *Silence of the Lambs*. We also purchased two police uniforms to be worn by Jacob and Ricky, who would bring Ivey to the cage.

The next stop was to find a dolly to complete the scene so that Ivey could be wheeled out. Eventually, we bought one at a pawnshop. We had all the props, except for one missing detail—entrance music. The music from *Silence of the Lambs* just was not that intimidating. After discussing a few horror themes, I pulled up the theme song from the movie *Saw* on my phone, and we decided that was perfect. Our mission was complete, and Team Ivey had a great time achieving it.

After returning to Kokomo, we went to the weigh-ins. Ivey had to pose for pictures with his opponent, who was mostly a stand-up kickboxer. He didn't like Ivey, and everyone could tell. The promoter, Mark Slater, said, "Both fighters can get their picture taken with the belt." Ivey declined and replied, "I will have plenty of time with the belt after the fight."

This match was important to both fighters. Both looked somewhat stressed, but Ivey had unwound much anxiety spending the weekend with friends. He was starting to joke and cut up, and that meant he was mentally ready for this fight. He looked over at the opponent's group he had with him and said with a smile, "I bet my team can beat up his team." I sized up his team and thought we could, but I hoped to avoid any complications on this trip, so I hoped that would not happen. Ivey was only joking. The tension around this fight was so thick I felt something could occur outside of the cage.

Ivey had decided he would win the title or retire. He was discouraged from the knockout in Japan, knowing that punch could have never hurt him just a few years ago. We had discussed this several times in the weeks leading up to the title fight; I was not sure if anyone knew of the decision except us, so I never mentioned the sensitive subject to anyone.

Ivey's opponent did not like to fight on the ground and was well aware that is where Ivey always wants the fight to be. Additionally, this was Ivey's opponent's hometown, and he understandably wanted to be the champion there. In many ways, an advantage with the hometown crowd on his side, but also a ton of pressure on him not to look bad. The man knew Ivey's fights are frequently won in the first round, and often in the first minute. To lose that way in front of your hometown crowd would be humiliating. Both men were coming off a critical loss. Expectations were building as both sides realized how bad the other needed this win.

We returned to the hotel; now it was time for the coaches and Ivey to unwind from the hype. For Chance and me, it was now time to do some interviews. We fast bonded as a team. I talked, and he filmed for his documentary at the same time. Chance would throw out questions he wanted on video sometimes from behind the camera. We kept everything very relaxed, as it seemed to help the communication with Ivey's type of crowd. Chance believes in filming it all and editing it later.

I met with Ivey's former girlfriend's parents, the Chandlers. Another surprising interview I felt awkward about doing. I was thinking, *If I were a celebrity, the last thing I would want is the scorned parents of a girl I broke up with getting their opinion of me broadcast in my biography or documentary.* Again, I was wrong. I not only got an informative interview, I also had an enjoyable time. I could see why Ivey loves them: they are people who create a comfort zone around themselves, which is perfect for Ivey's people anxiety issues.

They had requested that the interview be done in their hotel room. I was okay with that but wondered why. We knocked on their door and were let in by Robert Chandler. He had a beer in hand and seemed a little tipsy; his wife sat on the bed, behind his chair, where she gave suggestions and helped him answer a question. This couple was a classic case of a leading man backed by a strong woman in a great relationship. When Chance turned the camera on, Mr. Chandler asked if he needed to get rid of the beer, so it didn't get filmed. Chance said, "I am shooting above it."

The Chandlers were a perfectly matched couple; both were laid back, outspoken, and merry from the first moment. They were an in-depth interview. We covered Ivey's romantic life, friendships, career, parental skills, and just about everything else. Things never got boring; this couple knows Ivey from every angle. I knew Ivey considerably better when I walked out of their room than when I had entered.

Another interview while in Kokomo was with Chandler's cousin Fred Dulay, who was in Kokomo to corner for Ivey. He was Ivey's boxing coach. Once again, I found another astounding couple in Ivey's life. At this point, it became evident to me that Ivey surrounds himself with people who do not fit into statistical averages. He chooses exceptional individuals with outstanding personal qualities.

Fred is a hardworking man, as well as a boxing coach, but that is not what impressed me most. Statistically, the odds favored him being a failure in life, yet he had achieved a great deal. At a young age, things were stacked heavily against him; in his youth, his younger girlfriend became pregnant. At that time in the state of California, minors had to go to court to gain approval for marriage.

Fred was turned down by the judge, but he requested a meeting with the judge to attempt to reverse the decision. The judge informed him his decision was final; he believed in a year, the couple would divorce, and the young mother would become a statistic. Fred replied to the comment by saying, "So you are going to make her a statistic now instead?" The decision was reversed, and the marriage happened.

After years of hard work, Fred and his wife are still together and have a happy life. Fred had accomplished a lot in life and used his finances to open a boxing gym with one goal: to coach his son to become a pro boxer. Fred's son now has a perfect ten wins and no losses as a pro boxer. Recently, he stepped aside and allowed a more connected boxing coach to take over grooming and start aiming his son for a world title.

Fred had recently closed his boxing gym, with his son headed for higher levels and all goals achieved. Now he focused on Ivey's title fight. Fred had, over the years, taught Ivey, who was all grappler, to use boxing in his style, which is not an easy task. I am a grappler by nature, and in my experience, teaching a grappler to strike is like giving a cat swimming lessons.

Fred explained to me the strategy of Ivey shocking the opponent with a forward boxing style before taking him to the ground. I was worried about this plan, fearing Ivey might get knocked out during the approach to his opponent, but I had to agree, the stand-up fighter would never expect this. I reminded myself that Ivey is not easy to knock out and has gone the distance with UFC Hall of Fame fighters many times.

We returned to our room, and everyone was deep in thought. I wondered if I would sleep that night. I was stressed and exhausted. The next day was either going to be Ivey's last day as a fighter or the beginning of his new title reign. Still lurking in the shadows was the stress that his second card, which he was promoting, was just a week away; but he was trying hard not to think about that. Ivey put in a DVD, and everyone kicked back to fall asleep watching it.

Chance "Rich" Richardson, Jacob "the Killer" Kilburn, and Johnathan Ivey clowning around.

## JOHNATHAN IVEY: THE MAN BEHIND THE MONSTER

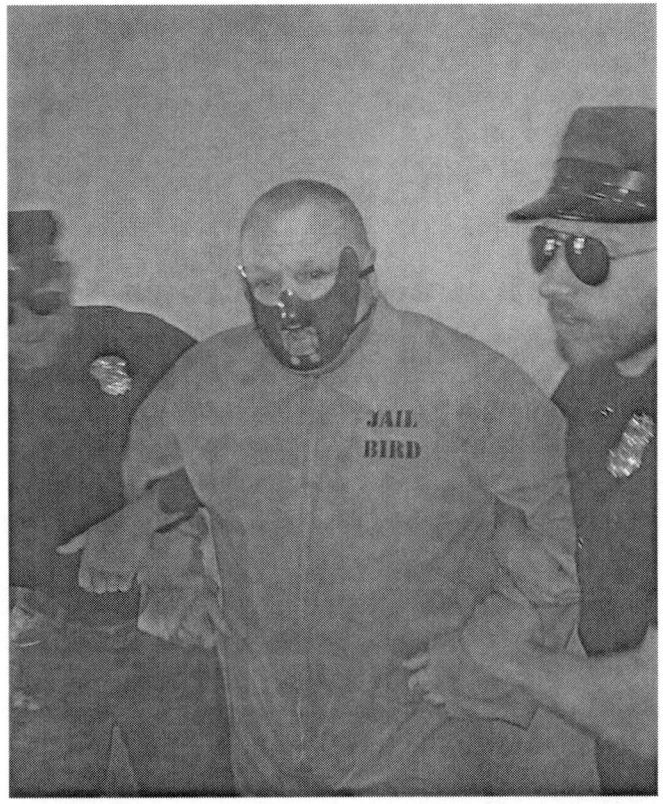

Ricky Ward and Jacob Kilburn practicing with Ivey for his big entrance.

CHAPTER 16

# Meeting Ivey's Crowd

*And let us consider one another in order
to stir up love and good works.*
—Hebrews 10:24 (NKJV)

I had made the trip to Kokomo to cover Ivey's title fight. Once there, the big surprise was how much I gained from meeting all his friends. Ivey and I had been friends for years, but now I know him. Before the trip was over, I felt I had looked inside of Ivey's soul and known him better than a brother. This random collection of people together showed me who Ivey was.

This trip was about me covering Ivey's title fight, but I used my counselor's experience far more than that of my MMA knowledge. Ivey's friends were all people who honored relationships far above normal commitment levels. They were the type who, if they loved you, they would never betray you. Over the years, Ivey had collected a very select crowd from whom he can draw strength, and those are the people he wanted around him the weekend of the fight.

Recently, I was meeting Ivey in Dickson, Tennessee, for one of our regular Friday nights. When I arrived, he mentioned how badly he needed to find the restroom. He had been in the parking lot waiting for forty-five minutes in his discomfort. To Ivey, that suffering was less than walking into a restaurant full of strangers alone. He hates to be alone, yet he prefers going solo over crowds of strangers. He prefers crowds of strangers over people he knows he cannot trust. It all makes sense when you think about it long enough. It also explains the complicated team he has assembled once you get to know them.

This learning process I experienced on this trip was a life lesson for me, being a loner. I have friends, but I have dependency issues. I am the guy friends can count on, not the one who relies on others. Johnathan was my exact opposite. His friends are his foundation. I admired the total trust he holds in them, and I hope someday to allow myself to have that.

I had often wondered how Ivey, a kid who more or less raised himself knowing nothing but fighting, turned out to be such a great person instead of a statistic. I got my answer on this trip. Ivey had over the years admired honorable people and developed those same qualities. Most of Ivey's better characteristics are also evident among his crowd. You might say he reversed peer pressure into a positive thing.

Fred Dulay, Ivey's boxing coach and close friend is a prime example of "Ivey's crowd." The group Ivey has assembled, known as Team Ivey consisted of boxing coach Fred Dulay, jiujitsu coach Ricky Ward, undefeated pro fighter Jacob Kilburn, tech wizard Chance Richardson, and myself. Fred traveled in last and chose to get himself a separate room, so he was the last one I met.

Fred and Ivey had met when Ivey was in a group that came in to negotiate establishing a boxing camp to train for cage fighting. Mixed martial arts has a broad range of fighting styles, but boxing is still a standard when the fight does not go to the ground. Ivey is all ground; he has won many times by striking, but his comfort zone is always on the ground. To be prepared, he trains in boxing, and Fred Dulay is a solid coach.

Fred is not a typical coach; he is much closer to the people he trains. For example, Thursday is Spaghetti night. His wife cooks and invites the athletes to be part of the family, so to speak.

Ivey distances himself from most people; he is polite, humble, and friendly with all non-aggressive personalities.

Aggressive personalities are in his danger zone.

The people he grows close with are a select group, mostly based on what most people would call honor, integrity, or trustworthiness. In short, the people who Ivey believes will never wrong him.

If they have that, he will overlook flaws most will not.

Fred made that cut to find himself in Ivey's inner circle of Team Ivey.

Fred became a dad too young. He built his whole life around his wife and his child, and in the process, he became successful both in life and in parenting. Like Ivey, Fred beat the odds doing what he must to be there for his family. No wonder Fred and Ivey are close. Though unlike in many ways, they share the same character of determination where it counts most. They do what they must for their loved ones, and they are good at it.

Like Ivey, Fred also made a family out of friends. During Spaghetti Thursday, when Ivey and other fighters from Fred's gym would gather together, they became closely bonded with the Dulays. The irony of this was that when I interviewed the Chandlers, they mentioned Johnathan coming to a similar night at their home, Taco Tuesday, for the same purpose. When I interviewed the two families back to back, I found specific patterns of behavior that leaped out at me.

When Fox and I were discussing the interviews, he noted that they were at first very informative, then highly repetitious. Ivey was so persistently, well, Ivey! If you talked to many people who all had a different take on someone or who had all different types of crowds, it would make you question who they in fact are. But the testimony of Ivey's companions and the distinct patterns, I knew beyond the shadow of a doubt who Ivey was.

Being a pro fighter is a hard path. I have known many. Success comes at a high price. They sacrifice friends, family, romances, and lifestyles to gain the next level. They often relocate, changing gyms, coaches, sponsors, and managers to better themselves as fighters. Sometimes the athletes must desperately influence promoters to get the big matches they need. Ivey is different; he never makes that kind of trade-off.

Ivey has his ways, and they involve total different views of priorities. When he negotiates a fight, he often takes less money to get more of his friends in the package. Ivey plans his career around his family. He never gives up the ones closest to him to get ahead. Perhaps this is one more reason why he has been overlooked by the icon promotions while he repeatedly proved he could hold his own against several fighters who stood in their coveted spotlights.

I have noticed that Ivey could have been much more successful if he had done things differently. For example, choosing a select crowd of influential people, training with big name fight teams who can offer higher paying opportunities, big contracts, a manager that had inside pull to make sure he gets the right fights that give him the advantage and get in with promoters who can take him all the way. Ivey doesn't suck up well to people of power and influence. He never, so to speak, plays well with others if they are not honorable people.

Many I interviewed stated precisely the same things I have observed. UFC vet Sean McCorkle said that if Ivey had the right manager there is no telling how far he could have gone. However, I doubt if Ivey would have ever traded friends, family, and lifestyle, even for a world title. That is not who Ivey is. On this trip, I saw why Ivey insists on surrounding himself with people who are real friends to him because he is so authentic himself he expects the same of others. The political end of the cage is not for Ivey.

Some of Ivey's crowd at Dick's Last Resort. (From left to right) Chance Richardson, Charlie Dykstra, Jacob Kilburn, Johnathan Ivey, Ricky Ward, Fred Dulay, and Robert Chandler.

# JOHNATHAN IVEY: THE MAN BEHIND THE MONSTER

Michael Fox, Savannah Ivey, Johnathan Ivey, and Charlie Dykstra visiting Lion of Judah Judo in Camden, Tennessee, shortly before leaving out for the Kokomo title fight.

## CHAPTER 17

# The Moment of Truth

*For a righteous man may fall seven times and rise again ...*
—Proverbs 24:16 (NKJV)

Fight day arrived fast, and the tension was building. I was watching Ivey close. I knew he was the better fighter, and I knew he might be forty-one, but he was still formidable in the cage. However, I was only worried about his emotional state entering this fight. When he was knocked out in Japan, he lost much confidence in himself. He knew he was not as physically capable of taking damage in his forties as he had been when younger.

I tried to psychoanalyze him but got nothing. He was a closed book on fight day. Sometimes he laughed and acted like there was no fight coming; other times he seemed deep in thought. But no pattern to his behavior. I had nothing to go on.

Everyone wanted to go back to Indianapolis, to eat lunch at Dick's Last Resort. I had never heard of the place. They explained it was a theme restaurant, where they treat you bad as part of the entertainment. Puzzled, I agreed to go, thinking, *Why do you want to eat where they mistreat you?* I am not big on long drives for short stops, as a person who values my time above most assets in my life, but I had hoped the trip would also pass the time quickly before the fight, and it did. Anything would be better than sitting around stressed out at the hotel.

We loaded up the SUV and headed back to Indianapolis. We sat in our regular places, the two quieter ones in the front, I drove, and

Chance was in the passenger seat. The louder personalities—Jacob, Ricky, and Ivey—were in the back. We arrived after the long ride and a lot of crazy conversation. It took a good bit of walking from the parking garage to get to Dick's.

We had arranged to meet there with more of Ivey's crowd, who had traveled to the title fight. I was observing Ivey's closest friends in group form now and gaining a compressed image of his lifestyle. These random personalities were showing me patterns. They were all informal, spoke their mind openly and honestly, and they were all loyal to those they cared about. That was what made people who were so different all fit so well together.

During the meal, everyone laughed and played along as we were insulted by the rude waiter. Michelle Chandler fired some attitude right back while smiling. Next, the same server made paper hats and wrote very degrading statements on them before placing the hat on the head of each person. The first one went on Jacob, and it read, "I am two inches from being a girl."

I was now curious to see if the waiter had the nerve to do this to Ivey. He did, but chose to do Ivey last and then quickly vanished before Ivey could read what he had written. Ivey's insult was, "I miss prison showers." Ivey was quite laid back about all of this, and the group had an enjoyable time. I later found out it was Ivey who initially requested we eat there.

Overshadowing the fellowship was the sobering thought that this day was potentially the last day of my friend Ivey's career. Everything I had studied told me there was no way, other than a lucky punch, that his opponent could beat him; but I have seen many lucky punches in this sport. I tried to ignore my worries and enjoy lunch.

The day passed by fast. Later in the day, Ivey chose an Italian restaurant for us to eat at for traditional reasons. He explained that he always eats spaghetti before his fights. I had studied recommended foods before fighting in a video by former UFC champion Marco Ruas, and spaghetti didn't make that list. However, I knew Ivey well enough to know whatever helped get his emotional state right for the fight was always best.

After a short rest back at the hotel, we went to the fights. We were running a little behind on purpose; Ivey always hates to be early. It was a long card, and we did a lot of waiting for the double main event to come. A fighter was injured, causing further delay.

The match drew close, and it was time to get the props ready. Ivey put on the prison jumpsuit, which he struggled to get over his massive shoulders. His concern would be that he would not be able to get it off when he got to the cage. After some practice, we figured out that if he looked downward while Ricky and Jacob pulled, the suit came right off.

Relaxing while they leaned him back on the dolly was hard for Ivey. He freaked out and jumped off the first few times in practice. It is not easy for Ivey to allow himself to give up control to others, but about the fourth time, he got the hang of it.

Later, Ivey put on the mask. It was now time. The music from *Saw* started, and my cue was to open the curtain when I heard the phrase "I want to play a game." I opened the curtain, and out came the two policemen wheeling a pumped-up version of Hannibal Lecter, and the crowd loved it.

Kokomo was Ivey's opponent's hometown, but Ivey was already winning the crowd. I heard several comments on our way to the cage. Some statements were unrepeatable as shocked crowd members marveled at the entrance. Some laughed or looked stunned, with eyes opened wide, but all were impressed.

On the way out to the cage, Mr. Chandler leaned over the barrier wall to encourage Ivey, who came out of character for that one moment, feeling inspired by the presence of someone he so admired. Everything could not have been more perfect.

As rehearsed, Ivey's outfit came off without a problem. He entered the cage and looked focused. He paced about like a caged lion. I had a good feeling he was about to be the champ.

The tension was thick as the ref, UFC vet Gary Copeland, prepared to start the fight. There was no doubt from the look on both fighter's faces that this was going to be over fast. It was hard for me to believe Ivey's fate would unfold in the next minute or two, but I knew it might not even take that long.

When Copeland signaled for the fight to begin, Ivey came out with a very aggressive forward movement but did not shoot in as he usually does. Ivey, just as boxing coach Fred Dulay predicted, threw a solid left, which landed hard, sending his opponent reeling backward. Next, Ivey clinched his opponent, preventing any striking, then pulled him down on top of himself! The livid adversary yelled at Ivey that he had messed up. I choose to leave the exact offensive quote out of his statement.

Long ago, it was thought that whoever was on top was winning. There is an advantage to having the dominant position, but not when a striker is on the ground with a legendary grappler. Ivey went right to work, attempting various leg locks. His opponent had stated that he was trained and ready for Ivey's leg locks, and his defense was excellent. Ivey began to transition from one attempt to another with blinding speed that was apparently shocking this striker. It was clear to all that he would remain on defense. Ivey would sooner or later snag his leg. If he stopped to hit Ivey, Ivey would have him in a submission. Soon Ivey snagged an ankle in an awkward position for both men, with him holding the ankle from the bottom while the opponent was cradled up trying to pin Ivey down.

Ivey was cranking the ankle severely, but the boxer was still somewhat positioned to hit Ivey. Ivey began cranking the ankle so hard it was making loud popping noises and doing severe damage, as the opponent unloaded punches to Ivey's head. I had no view of Ivey's face from my corner, leaving me wondering how hurt he was by the blows. I saw blood and knew it was Ivey's. He was bleeding around his eye. I was unsure if he was getting close to being knocked out before he could finish the submission; the entire coliseum had no doubt this would end in seconds but could go either way. For those few seconds, time seemed to go into slow motion.

The ankle made a series of about six loud pops, and on the last pop, the fighter yelled out in pain. In MMA, yelling out loud is called a verbal submission, or a verbal tap. Referee Gary Copeland dove in and stopped the fight, preventing further damage. The opponent shot backward, scrambling to get away from Ivey.

The fight lasted just over a minute. Ivey was the new champion. His career would continue. He proved that he could still take a punch by getting hit many times. It all happened so fast, but the tension had made that one of the most extended minutes of my entire life!

Now I knew his career was not over. All spirits were high as we started our way back to the locker room to see the doctor. Ivey looked pretty banged up. He was bloody and had much swelling around his eye. I asked him if he was ever near to getting knocked out, and he said, "No, it didn't even hurt that bad. I knew it was about to be over, and I didn't want to give up his ankle, so I just let him hit me while I got the lock on." Leave it to Ivey to have a plan for victory that scared us all half to death!

It wasn't the first time Ivey had done any of that, pulling a fighter on top of him to open a potential submission or let the opponent hit on purpose. Ivey is not there to win points for judges' decisions; he comes to submit his opponents at all cost.

When we got Ivey back to the locker room, some small children snuck in behind us and asked me if they could see Ivey. I led them back to him, and Ivey gladly received them. Bloody and swollen, he posed for pictures with the kids.

Many fans had switched from cheering for their hometown hero to cheering for Ivey that night. Years ago in MMA, there were no rounds, or points, or judges in the sport; it was called no holds barred (NHB). Back then, someone won, and someone lost, and the fights were frequently short and energetic. Many fans preferred that. Ivey most often entertains the crowd using an NHB game plan in the sport of MMA, adding to that his ring entrances and crazy entertaining moves and the people get a great show for their money. Often, this turns critics into Ivey supporters.

Unfortunately, not everyone was happy about Ivey's win. After a short bit of celebrating and Ivey getting paid for the fight, an official from the sanctioning body came to warn us that a local gang was making death threats. It seemed they were unhappy with the fight's outcome and now were starting to cause trouble. The woman looked me straight in the eye and said: "You need to leave now!"

I agreed. The last thing we need is violence at a show to harm the sport. The parking for the fighters and coaches was behind the building; we left unnoticed and without incident.

The night was unforgettable. Ivey said to me when it was just us, "I guess we got the happy ending we need for the biography."

I replied to him, "Yeah, next we will sell out your second show."

Ivey had put the stress of the show out of his mind, but now it was time to go back to work. In seven days, he had to go from fighter to promoter, which was devastatingly stressful last time. I could see in his eyes that Ivey believed the happy ending was coming. He once again believed in himself.

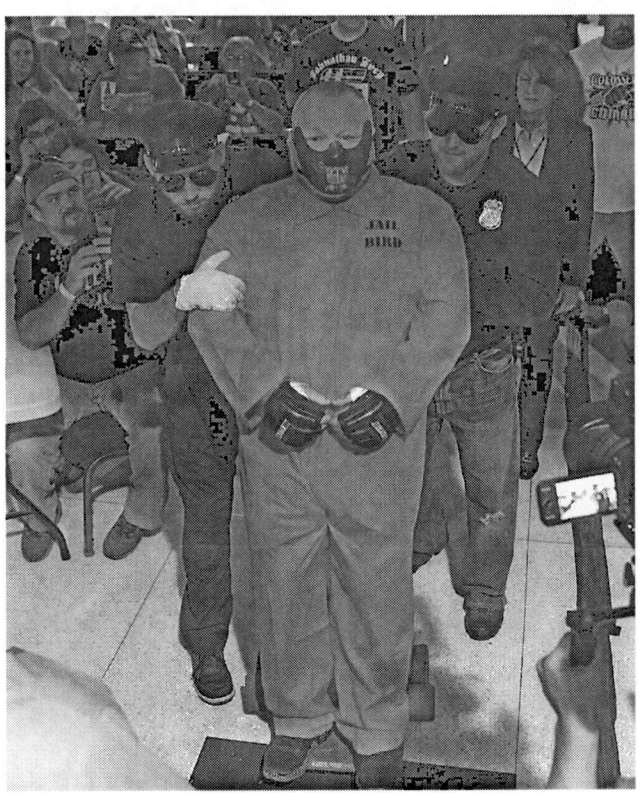

Ivey being brought to the ring by Jacob and Ricky, amazing the crowd by the entrance!

Ivey, a champion at forty-one years old!

## CHAPTER 18

# Ivey's Second Show: The Other Moment of Truth

> A faithful man will abound with blessings,
> But he who hastens to be rich will not go unpunished.
> —Proverbs 28:20 (NKJV)

After all the hard work that Ivy put into both the title fight and his second show, I knew there would be a happy ending. Ivey prepared mentally in the same week he recovered physically from the cage. When the night of weigh-ins came, he still looked banged up.

Ivey had suffered mostly tissue damage around his eye, but also a subconjunctival hemorrhage. There was visible blood under the surface of his eye. He sought no medical help due to the absence of health insurance. As far as the appearance, it only added to his tough guy image. One fighter who had some facial bruises posed for a picture with Ivey clowning around.

This show was different; there was stress, but not like last time. Ivey had sold out all twenty-five private tables and many advanced seats. He was not sure he would sell out this larger venue, but he was no longer worried about losing money on the higher-cost event.

Ivey was comfortable with me as the ISKA rep, Yonah Yisrael as the well-experienced referee, and the best ringside doctor I know, Albert Bystritkii, who is native Russian. We all meshed well; making Ivey comfortable solves most of his anxiety-based problems.

Weigh-ins on Friday night went smoothly, with everyone making weight. One fighter could not make it to weigh-ins but was underweight at fight time anyway, whereas most competitors made weight and then gained back considerably before the fight.

We suffered only small frustrations, which are inevitable in this sport. The lone letdown on the fight card was Tommy Scrivner, who was not released from jail in time to fight. But the card had enough matches without that one missing fight.

With bell time only two hours away, we held the rules meeting. Anthony Maness had stressed safety as the priority to me since I was a new ISKA rep. There had been a recent card in Kentucky where an athlete died following his fight. I do not believe the Kentucky rules had anything to do with the tragedy, but Kentucky, unlike Tennessee, allows more dangerous moves such as excessive slamming, foot stomps, and knees to the head. We had several fighters on this card who had competed in Kentucky and would need reminding of the rules.

During the rules meeting, Jacob Kilburn from Harris Holt, who often fights in Kentucky, asked if foot stomping was legal. Dr. Albert Bystritskii and I both replied—"No!"—at the same time. It was a relief to have a doctor who knew as much as any qualified ISKA rep, to back me since I was a rookie. I cited the rule by number. The copy of the ISKA rules had that one highlighted. There was no argument, and no foot stomping happened that night.

With about an hour and a half to go, the lines began to form. It looked like another sellout. Once the doors opened, the crowds poured in, and soon the building reached capacity.

The first show was excellent for a new promoter. This show had hundreds more than the first, way more professionally done and had a much better card. Ivey had taken it to the next level and sold the show out doing it.

Ivey's matchmaking skill impressed me most. At first, I was doubtful. I was worried that he was focusing too much on ticket selling matchups and might sacrifice quality, ending up with many short one-sided fights. I knew as soon as I saw the completed card that it could not be any better all around. The show was awesome.

Once again, Ivey transformed into the promoter everyone wanted to see when the lights dimmed and the music started. Ivey came in, appearing in a flashy suit with a matching hat. He had put it on just before the show's start. Everyone laughed but were impressed with the look. Ivey had the celebrity something about him to get away with the striking apparel. I heard a comment that "anyone else would look like a pimp, but it looks good on him!" He was more than adapting to this business; he was enjoying it.

There were a few misfortunes on that night. One fighter, Chaz Jordan, received an extreme eye gouge in the first few seconds of the fight resulting in being unable to compete. The eyelid tore, and the eyeball was injured as well. Fortunately, he did not lose his sight and will fully recover.

Another fighter, Michael Frey, injured his shoulder on a takedown. The rugged Frey managed to finish out the round with injury but was not able to continue after an examination between rounds. He too is recovering well.

My friend Desean Wolf had a garment malfunction. Bluntly put, Desean's cup kept falling out; the rules state that competitors must wear protective gear. His friends formed a circle of privacy around him cage side, so his desperate corner man could duck tape the cup to his body since this was the only option to prevent forfeiting the fight.

The distracted fighter lost the match and several patches of body hair in the process. I felt for Desean, but he did add comical relief to Ivey's show. Later, he was laughing it off and is now looking forward to returning to redeem his pride.

These few difficulties were minimal compared to the issues at most MMA events. There are so many factors to these events that even pay-per-view shows with millions of dollars invested have experienced far worse happenings.

The crowd was pleased with both Ivey and the experience; there was no doubt in anyone's mind that Johnathan Ivey's Cage Fighting Championships was here to stay. Many times I looked around the packed house and felt surreal. How did Ivey pull off so much by only his second show?

He had been building a reputation since August of 1998; in his nineteen-year career, he proved himself. Now people expected shows to be remarkable if Ivey put it on, and he met their expectations fully. You could say he spent nineteen years making this show happen; it was not a hasty whim out of desperation for money, it was the revelation of his life's work.

When the show ended, Ivey walked around to thank every person who had helped in any way. He had a long night of cleaning up and folding up chairs ahead, but he took care of personal business first. I helped as much as I could, but I had a van full of people waiting to travel two hours to get home. When I loaded my equipment that we used in the show, Ivey handed me a bank bag; it contained the repayment of the loan I gave him. He then said, "Thanks for believing in me more than I believed in myself!" He expressed his appreciation for taking a chance on him. I pointed out that it would only be taking a chance if there was a risk of failure, and there never was any such risk.

Caleb Miller's postfight photo with Ivey at Ivey's second show.

## CHAPTER 19

# From Monster to Mentor

*Do not be overcome by evil, but overcome evil with good.*
—Romans 12:21 (NKJV)

Ivey has overcome far more than opponents; he has conquered the statistical odds stacked against him. In this process, Ivey has become a role model to many who need to do the same. He has a great deal of positive influence to offer, empowered with his charisma, which has such an impact.

Ivey is a man they call a monster; he is feared and respected. Despite his intimidating reputation and appearance, he is not comfortable around people. He fights those fears, to reach out to people whenever he thinks he can make a difference.

In his humility, Ivey refuses to call anyone fans. He hates the way that sounds. He said if he tries to call his supporters fans, it makes him feel like a douchebag. He calls them supporters because they support him and he is always humbled by the appreciation from each one of them. I have never met a celebrity of any form so moved by those who looked up to him. He views his supporters as what makes him and why he is. He sees his whole life revolving around them, instead of the other way around. That self-image positively redefines the entire fighter overview, for many youths involved in combat sports. These young people badly need that kind of mentor.

The wrongful self-image of a tough guy often leads young athletes into big trouble. Ivey discourages that behavior every chance he gets, recalling his troubled youth as a motive. My experience in coaching amateur MMA has left me all too aware of how many young people with behavior problems need positive influences like Johnathan Ivey in their lives.

I took the following clip from Ivey's Facebook to show the type of example he tries to set:

> *Facebook!! If you're a young dude and you've ever for any reason looked at me with respect or valued my opinion about anything, let me talk to you for a second. I want to share something with you that I wish someone that I respected would have shared with me when I was coming up ... Build your life strong. Fill your heart with love. Fill your heart with kindness. With patience, with humbleness. You know ... that is what makes a powerful man. All that gangsta stuff "I don't take crap from anybody" and all that type mentality. That will just put you in a cage or a casket. That's not what strong men do. Strong men forgive, strong men apologize, strong men take care of their family with love and kindness and gentleness. That's how you build strength. And if at all possible stay away from drugs, they make it to hard to stay focused. It's hard to hang out with the right people when you're just worried about getting high. I love each one of you; I don't want you to add roadblocks and hurdles to your path. I wish you all the best. Keep grinding young dudes!! Our future needs you. #Love"*

Ivey and I have a mutual acquaintance through MMA, namely, Tommy Scrivner, a fighter I coached a short while back when he was only fifteen years old is a prime example of such troubled youths. Tommy was very likable, determined, and had a ton of heart. Much like Ivey, he had a shortage of positive influence in his life, he was temperamental, and quick to fight.

## JOHNATHAN IVEY: THE MAN BEHIND THE MONSTER

While still underage, Tommy falsified his age and became a cage fighter at only sixteen, two years before it was legal in the state of Tennessee. Ironically, he debuted against someone about as honest as he is. His opponent was foreign and debuting as an amateur, in America. Later, it was learned he had fought professional levels overseas. Tommy took a loss, but it never slowed him down.

Ivey and Tommy met when Ivey was the referee of one of Tommy's early matches. Ivey took one look at Tommy and was suspicious of his age. Ivey said, "You're young. If you're in trouble, I am going to have to step in early." Tommy was offended. He snapped a quick reply, "Let me get beat stupid, but don't stop this fight!" Ivey connected to Tommy right away; he saw himself in Tommy.

That same night, Tommy had to fight a more experienced and larger opponent because there was no one his size or level. The fight went the distance, and Tommy, at age sixteen, won the judges' decision against the bigger man.

After the fight, Tommy asked Ivey for an autograph. When Ivey signed it, he wrote an encouraging note that said, "Monkeys can't hang with gorillas!" Ivey became Tommy's hero and role model. To this day, Tommy says he wants to be just like Johnathan Ivey.

Tommy eventually was caught fighting underage, resulting in the ISKA suspending him. He was devastated; he had lost the one thing that gave him a purpose in his life. I recall seeing Tommy watch, but not participate, in an event. He looked as sad as if it were a funeral. It was not in Tommy to watch MMA; he wanted back in the cage.

The suspension was not the end of Tommy fighting in the cage, however, with his level of determination. Tommy was determined to find grappling matches, which often were used to patch holes in cards when needed. These are considered exhibitions since there is no punching or kicking. He did many, even one against me, calling me, his former coach out with the challenge.

After some rule searching, Tommy discovered he could legally be a kickboxer. So if it were legal to kickbox in a ring, why not do it in a cage? Tommy spoke with promoters and talked them into adding "Caged Kickboxing" to their MMA shows whenever they need to fill out their card. Soon it caught on, and many matchmakers had added such matches. Tommy was far better at MMA, but at least he was back in the cage.

Just like Ivey in his youth, Tommy hit misfortune every time things started going well. Tommy relocated with his mother to an area that had no nearby MMA gym. With no gym to work out aggression, Tommy seemed to become much more volatile. Trouble appeared to find Tommy unless Tommy discovered it first. He got involved in drugs as well as other legal complications. He was precisely the kind of young man who needed someone like Ivey for a mentor.

Tommy got word that Johnathan Ivey had started promoting MMA shows, and he was determined to return to fighting. His goal was to win a fight on Ivey's show by leg lock in honor of Johnathan Ivey's legacy. Still training independently, he was a considerable underdog against the only available opponent who was from a well-respected team, Harris Holt.

Ivey agreed to put Tommy on the card on his first event, and the two spoke a lot online. Ivey had just started encouraging Tommy to stay clean when Tommy got into trouble. Tommy was in jail, and it appeared he would not be able to fight.

I gave Ivey the bad news, and the fight card was the least of his worries. Ivey blamed himself, thinking had he taken a bit more time to encourage Tommy, it would not have happened. Ivey cares about people; he hates to see anything negative happen to anyone.

Fortunately, Tommy got released in time for the fight. Ivey lined him up for a radio interview and introduced him to the spotlight. Thanks to Ivey, he was finding his purpose. It all looked good again.

The event rolled around, and Tommy seemed cursed with bad luck. He ran out of gas just a few miles from the venue but managed to get help in time to make it there. Tommy arrived late and stressed.

When it came time for his fight, he opened up with an intense head kick that looked perfect until he found himself slipping in some sweat on the mat and crashing down. Tommy's opponent took control of Tommy instantly, capitalizing on the slip. The stronger man having Tommy's back, eventually, choked Tommy out.

Tommy referred to this as his Charlie Brown loss, calling to mind the cartoon character slipping on his attempt to kick a football. He was determined to return to the cage on Ivey's next event. Ivey knew all too well the discouragement Tommy was feeling and the determination to prove himself. He set Tommy to fight on the second card against an opponent nearly perfectly matched with himself. Tommy was inspired and ready.

All looked well again, but Tommy's opponent pulled out of the fight. Ivey rematched him with an old rival, Brannon Philips, Tommy's former teammate. They had fought before several times, and it was always a great matchup. This opportunity was Tommy's big chance to become known in the sport.

Then came the tragedy. Tommy got arrested for attempted murder and held with a sizable cash-only bond. His mother contacted me when she was unable to reach Ivey. She explained that Tommy asked her to make sure she got word to us both. He was facing a long-term prison sentence, but his biggest concern was not letting Ivey down by failing to show up for his match! That is the kind of influence Ivey has as a mentor.

Tommy settled the charges in time but, sadly, missed his match. He was facing thirty-eight years but made an excellent plea deal agreeing to one hundred and fifty days and no felony record.

Ivey decided to put him on the third card, which will take place early next year. I gave Tommy the news, and he was excited. Tommy got a job and went back to training. As we talked, I mentioned the biography; he knew nothing about it because of his incarceration.

He jokingly said to mention him in it. I laughed, and then I explained about doing a chapter on Ivey as a mentor, which he would fit in perfectly. However, I cautioned him my coverage of his situation would somewhat exploit the scandals in his life. After explaining, I asked if he was all right with that. He said, "I am negotiating to go on *Jerry Springer*. Of course, I am okay with being exploited!" So we agreed to an interview at T Birds restaurant in Lexington, Tennessee.

About an hour before the interview, I got a text from Tommy asking if he could bring a date. I replied that was fine, but reminded him we would be discussing him trying to kill his former girlfriend's new boyfriend. I felt that would be awkward for the new girl. Tommy replied, "Well yeah, that's the thing ... It is kinda the same girl." I was stunned.

When the interview happened, I, like Ivey, encouraged them to stay out of trouble, and both agreed they had enough of the rough life. He had learned his lesson while stressing over the thought of spending thirty-eight years in prison. He had rethought things while reading the Bible to pass the time.

Tommy explained how he got into so much trouble. He got jumped by two guys who broke his nose, and he wanted revenge. Dressed in all black, Tommy took a baseball bat to one of their houses. After smashing all of the security cameras, he began to break down the front door and found himself dodging bullets. After a short police chase and an arrest, Tommy bailed out of jail.

He would be out only two days, before his next arrest. The guy who now liked the girl he was broken up with at the time, attempted to run him off the road. After the first bump the truck gave him, he was able to regain control of his car, but the second bump crashed his car. Tommy had been hunting and had a shotgun loaded with slugs. His doors would not open, so he used the sunroof and fired a shot through the back window of the truck. He explained that he missed the driver's head but got himself charged with two counts of attempted murder.

I asked "Two?"

Tommy said, "Yeah she was in there too." He pointed at his girlfriend. The girl sitting beside him at the table, Hailey, had been shot at by Tommy!

I asked her, "What did you think when he shot at you!?"

She replied, "I thought he must love me." Her interpretation of the violent act was it was the passion of true love.

Many would give up on Tommy as just being a trouble-bound repeat offender. The determined Johnathan Ivey wanted to continue to interact with Tommy and try to guide him to a more stable life; Ivey has offered to assist him with his future MMA career if he would like to relocate to the Nashville area.

## JOHNATHAN IVEY: THE MAN BEHIND THE MONSTER

There are many other cases of Ivey mentoring in small and yet significant ways. One night I was going to meet up with Ivey and visiting my mother before I went. She was telling me about a relative helping an underprivileged child with a school project. The project consisted of creating a cartoon character, then mailing the figure from place to place for a vacation. The student then gathered pictures from the adventure and wrote a report on the details. The child had sent my mother her character and was going to write about Tennessee, and she needed ideas to help the little girl.

I took the character to Ivey, who gladly wrote a letter of encouragement to the girl and posed for a picture with the vacationing personality, then autographed him. The child reported on the sport of MMA and how the character she created spent time with a legendary fighter on vacation to Tennessee. With her autograph, letter, and photos she both got an A+ and won the school district competition with her project.

In another case, there was a nine-year-old kickboxer from Harris Holt MMA, nicknamed "Bam Bam," who was about to have his first kickboxing match. Word got to Ivey that his dream was to have Ivey corner for him. Sadly, Ivey was not able to do it, for reasons of scheduling, so he sent a video of encouragement instead.

Later Ivey heard the boy had lost the match, but there was to be a rematch. Ivey was staying in Paris, Tennessee, at the time of the rematch visiting relatives. He cut the visit short and drove to the event to corner for the young fighter. With his dream come true and his hero in his corner, the encouraged young boy won his rematch.

Ivey has a tender heart and is always looking to make a difference in others' lives. Once when we were eating at a restaurant, the waitress said: "Bear with me, it is my first day of work, and you two are the first order I have ever taken." Ivey left her a letter of encouragement and a twenty-dollar tip. He saw it as a perfect way to get her off to a good start on her new job.

Jacob Kilburn met up with Ivey at one of the leg lock seminars taught by Ivey, back when Jacob was an amateur. He was warned by MMA coach Lance Boyd not to joke with Ivey. Ivey and Jacob are an odd clash of personality types, but they bonded somehow. Now, of course with Jacob being a professional fighter, they corner for each other's fights and train together. When I interviewed Jacob, he mentioned Ivey surprising him with a gift of encouragement, which was a pair of Air Force One tennis shoes. Jacob had casually mentioned his shoes which he had been wearing since high school, Ivey jumped at the chance to give him a gift he would remember and created an inspirational mentoring moment.

One of my favorite mentor moments was when Ivey entered the Clash of the Champions Grappling Tournament, which had a cash prize. Ivey cares nothing about trophies; he always sells them, and he was there only looking to make some money to pay the bills. Ivey won the contest and received not only the cash prize but also a gold championship belt. As he was leaving, a starry-eyed child ran up to him to get his hero's autograph. He signed the autograph but also handed the child the gold belt! The mother protested, saying it was too valuable of a gift, and she would not allow the child to accept it. Ivey explained that he hopes that belt might encourage the boy to work hard for his goals. The overwhelmed mother allowed the excited child to take home the prize.

Ivey has a reputation for being a monster who has broken people's bones. He fights in a steel cage. His appearance frightens people. Few would guess he is a tenderhearted Christian man who looks for opportunities to impact the lives of so many people.

Tommy Scrivner and mentor Johnathan Ivey.

Ivey's tournament championship belt, which he gave to a child who asked for his autograph!

CHAPTER 20

# God Was Always There

> And we know that all things work together
> for good to those who love God,
> to those who are the called according to His purpose.
> —Romans 8:28 (NKJV)

Not everything that happens to those who love God is good, but we have the promise that all things work together for good. Johnathan Ivey looks back at his troubled life and understands now why so many bad things happened for a good reason. Ivey learned that God was always there. When we discussed this topic, the first thing that came to his mind was the drive-by shooting. He had planned to do the drive-by with the help of his buddies and left out on the mission only to have car trouble. The breakdown prevented a great tragedy. Some would call that a coincidence, but if so it was a life-saving one. Not only the life of potential victims but Ivey's as well.

That one event was more than evident. However, what if a long list of other things never happened? So many random factors created the Leg Lock Monster. Chance meetings introduced him to MMA. Random circumstances caused the chance meetings. Trying to analyze the providence of God is a strenuous exercise to the imagination, but a good one for our faith. It lets us know that we are being watched out for, even when it doesn't seem like it.

Ivey looks back at one time being court-ordered into anger management classes. He did not want to go, but as it turned out, the counselor was a preacher who became a friend and constructive spiritual influence in Ivey's life. Without Ivey going to anger management, the two would never have met.

Ivey's love for bench pressing started a chain reaction. First, it got him known at the gym, then he won a competition, and that gained him the attention of MMA champion Tommy Graham. Graham introduced him to the sport of MMA.

Blessings are not limited to what we can see. So many potential seeds of opportunity in Ivey's life are there, in which he may have only scratched the surface. The chance meeting in a restaurant in Dover, Tennessee, with the director of White Door Productions was one of them. Director Joseph Drake was one of my last interviews.

Like most, his first impression of Ivey was intimidating, which is not a bad thing, when you are making a horror movie. Since Joseph cast Ivey as himself in that film, I had to ask his thoughts. He explained that Ivey was great to work with and was careful not to hurt David G Baker, the actor who had to fill in for the stuntman in the fight scene. In every way, Ivey is just a natural at keeping the filming going smooth. He even came up with helpful suggestions for the film, including a location for his final scene. Harris Holt's gym in Clarksville Tennessee was used in the movie after Ivey suggested the ominous view of the killer walking through the hall visible through a glass wall from the main room. Joseph mentioned Ivey knows horror! His knowledge could come into play in the future.

Joseph gave a long list of potential roles Ivey was capable of playing, including, of course, a fighter, especially himself. Joseph also mentioned Ivey would make a great man behind the mask, speaking about the slasher in a horror film. He suggested that Ivey's soft-on-the-inside characteristic broadened his potential considerably. One role stood out that Joseph mentioned, in particular, a Mafia Lord. Ivey has said his dream role was to play Deathrattle, the demon-possessed mafia hitman from one of my books. It would appear God has blessed Ivey with a variety of potential roles. At forty-one years old, his MMA career is nearing the end, but as an actor, he could have decades ahead of him.

On the list, Ivey mentions is the day of his first show, when he was falling apart, and a preacher he had never met came up and said: "God told me to come talk to you." That moment helped Ivey hold together in one of the most trying days of his life. It is hard to say precisely why and who did what and what was their motives. We could spend tons of time trying to figure out what all is and is not the providence of God. However, we become more spiritual the day we accept and appreciate the fact that it is beyond us to fully know or understand him and just live by faith.

It is likely advisable not to ponder it too deeply, but things happen, and accept that they happen for a reason, and the purposes benefit us. So let us be thankful that we are being watched over and allow our faith to grow because of it.

What is the biggest challenge to our faith, is trusting it is for the best when bad things happen. Most of the time, we cannot recognize the future results coming from the current suffering in our lives. God can see all the way both directions, past and future. We can only see presently and hold on to a few memories of the past.

Ivey faced many discouragements in his life. Finally, now he is starting to see a forty-one-year plot unfold in the story that is his life. It was there all along, but we must live it through to see the outcome. This battle is far from unique to Johnathan Ivey; every person has this challenge.

An interesting thing happened about the time Ivey was trying to straighten up his spiritual life. His closest friend, Sam Taylor, invited him to a Terry Terrel gospel concert. Ivey never heard of Terry Terrel, but agreed and went along. During the performance, Terrel paused and pointed Ivey out in the crowd, calling everyone's attention to him. The spotlight had nothing to do with Ivey being a fighter. Terrel said, "God is going to use this man." Terrel never said why he said this and did not elaborate on the topic, but the short words of encouragement stuck in Ivey's mind from that day until now. Ivey sincerely hopes to be a positive influence on others.

God has already used Ivey in many ways. From blessing Savannah with a caring dad and so many others with an encouraging role model. He has helped people financially, emotionally, inspirationally, and many other ways. If we try to create a list, we limit the potential with our imagination. It is best to let God do His work continually and have faith in the big picture created by someone far surpassing ourselves.

When Ivey and I first discussed this book, he hoped that it might have an angle that affects some readers spiritually. That goal of Ivey's will be decided in the heart of the individual reader. Each of us has a free will and potential faith.

Take away the fame, the gold championship belts, and other exteriors of the Leg Lock Monster, and Johnathan Ivey is a man struggling through this world like each of us. Like any Christian, Ivey is a sinner saved by grace and has lived each day depending on God. Perhaps as people read, they can find common ground with him like so many Ivey supporters have. They may see themselves in him and, in one way or another, find needed inspiration.

Up-and-coming director Joseph A. Drake, who had a chance meeting with Johnathan Ivey and cast him into a role playing himself.

Ivey's love for horror movies made him perfect for his first roll, playing himself in a slasher film.

Ivey poses for pictures at the premiere of the movie *Fearsville 2*.

CHAPTER 21

# Where Do We Go from Here?

He who did not spare His own Son, but delivered Him up for us all, how shall He not with Him also freely give us all things?
—Romans 8:32 (NKJV)

For Johnathan Ivey, his forty-first year has been a blessed one. In the past, he did not believe he would be alive in a few years. His expectation for the future was poverty if he lived. Now Ivey is a successful promoter, and once again a heavyweight champion. He fought and won two huge battles. He has a hopeful future. But where do we go from here?

Next year, he will be another year older; and a few years after that, Savannah will need to go to college. The fact is there will always be another fight—perhaps it will be in the cage or out, maybe it will be physical, financial, emotional, mental, or spiritual. Who knows what tomorrow holds for us all? But the same God who was there the past forty-one years will always be there in the future.

It turns out Ivey is not so different from the rest of us after all. I have always believed the loyalty of Ivey's supporters comes from the fact that somehow they all see themselves in him. My sincere hope is that all who read this book will recognize that. He is no more or less vulnerable than us, and he struggles just like the rest of us. He beat the odds, and so can we.

Most of all, Ivey is as dependent on God as anyone else. Half the battle is over when we all realize that fact. Johnathan has accepted that dependency and hopes that somehow he can influence others to do the same.

We now end the story of the Man Behind the Leg Lock Monster, not because it is over, but because we have reached the present time on our timeline. God only knows where we go from here. Our faith tells us it will be all for the best.

For those who are curious about the future, I can throw out a few clues of where things might be going. The following paragraphs are some updated facts about Ivey and various members of his crowd. It may contain curiosities and teasers about what could unfold.

Ivey's next show is in the planning stage now. After his proven excellence as a promoter, it is hardly a mystery. I have no doubt it will be a smashing success.

The troubled young man Tommy Scrivner, who Ivey tries to influence to overcome his struggles, seems to be doing just that. He is now a forklift operator for a company that is shorthanded. Tommy works forty-five to seventy hours per week and is drawing a lot of over time. He is too busy and too tired to get into trouble. The company has agreed to help him get his certification as an operator, which will put him at a much higher pay level.

Tommy will be returning to the cage in February of next year. His opponent, ironically, is scheduled to be Desean Wolf, the fighter who had the garment malfunction at Ivey's second show. Desean's body hair has grown back from the duck tape incident, and he is looking forward to his chance to redeem himself after his misfortunate first appearance on Ivey's show. He stressed the fact that he will have new gear for this show.

I wish both young men the best of luck. Though both fighters cannot win, perhaps they can both impress enough people to make a name for themselves. It would be a blessing if it could be a split decision and the best fight of the night.

Savannah is the same humble near perfect child as ever. She is still Ivey's top priority. Ivey recently sent me a photo of Savannah at the circus. In the picture, had Savannah and a guest with her, Michael, the little boy who referred to Ivey as "the Johnathan who

## JOHNATHAN IVEY: THE MAN BEHIND THE MONSTER

loves me." Ivey is back interacting in the boy's life, and so far Ramona, Michael's mother approves.

Ramona, the girl that got away, recently went through a hard time with a personal disaster, and Ivey was there for her, coming to help in her time of need. No, they are not back together, but they are on peaceful terms, so who knows? It is, at the very least, progress.

I spoke just today with movie director Joseph Drake from White Door Productions. Joseph mentioned he is beginning a series called *The Hunt*. On the list of characters is one written to be played by Johnathan Ivey. There is also a feature film in the works for 2018, in which Joseph said: "I am sure you might be seeing Ivey's face in there somewhere!" The sly Mr. Drake is not about to give away secrets, but he has me curious. With what he speaks of Ivey's potential, I suspect a significant role could soon come Ivey's way.

Jacob "the Killer" Kilburn recently took his first loss. We all wondered how hard it might be for him when it finally happened. Relentless as ever, he was not discouraged, and he signed up for his next match right away. That fight will take place next month, and as a fellow member of Team Ivey, I wish him the very best!

As for former world kickboxing champion Anthony Maness, he and Ivey are still good friends. Anthony speaks very well of Ivey despite that slight brotherly flare-up the two had over Ivey's second show. I interviewed Anthony as the final interview for this biography, and he expressed his concern for Ivey continuing to fight while in his forties, recommending retirement from MMA and work in other areas, such as refereeing or an administrative position.

Anthony himself fought for the last time at forty-seven years old and won the fight. He was six years older than Ivey currently is, but that could be the motive behind his concern for Ivey. Anthony now requires antiseizure medication and is sure the damage from his final fight is the reason. He wants his friend Johnathan Ivey to retire to avoid suffering similar complications.

As for me, the experience of interacting with Johnathan Ivey has inspired me to step out of my ultra-practical lifestyle and chase some of my dreams. After this biography goes to the publisher, I will take a brief rest and then work on finishing all my other books. My fear of failure held me back until now, but I have replaced it with my fear of failing to try. That is the direct result of seeing my inspiration, Johnathan Ivey, face his fears.

As for Johnathan Ivey's inner struggles, he is thriving in most ways, and he is always growing as a person. Ivey recently learned that another promoter has been sabotaging him by stirring up the athletic commission. It seems when Ivey put on the first show, there was one small permit of which Ivey was unaware. The competitor had searched the public records to find fault with Ivey and then indicating to the athletic commission if they do not take action against Ivey, that it would be favoritism. I am betting the same promoter called the fire marshal on Ivey's first show. Ivey restrained himself from adding a twenty-fourth assault to his list while paying a two-hundred-and-fifty-dollar fine for the oversight.

Ivey is choosing not to attend the shows the man puts on to avoid being tempted to let the monster out of the cage one last time, which proves him wise. Sometimes the best form of self-control is disallowing the temptation ever to test you. To show my support for Ivey, I will not be attending this man's events either, despite the fact I have friends on the card.

This past Friday night, Fox and I met Ivey for dinner in Dickson. Upon arriving, I knew something was wrong. Ivey got out of his car and had a strained look on his face. As we walked toward the front doors, he kept looking back over his shoulder as if fighting an urge to turn around and go back. He finally told me the guy in the truck next to him had opened his door and hit Ivey's car very hard. The man made no apology and acted arrogantly about it. Ivey had restrained himself, something a few years back he would never have done. The arrogant man in the truck has no idea how fortunate he is that Ivey has grown that much as a person. Turning the other cheek is perhaps one of the hardest Bible teachings for us to follow, but Ivey did just that. He defied his very nature.

I pointed this out to Ivey, and he agreed that he did the right thing but said it was a struggle for him. I laughed and told him, "This is going in chapter 21! It fits perfectly!" His mood seemed to improve right away. Sometimes we all need to be reminded that our trials are often just victories waiting to happen. Quite frequently, if we can resist the urge to do anything at all, we have already won.

There is always another level to grow into, another battle to win, but no one can deny the growth of Johnathan Ivey. The monster that I watched throw a fighter across the cage all those years ago was undeniably strong, but the man behind the monster is even stronger.

The Monster ...

# CHARLIE DYKSTRA

… and the man behind the Monster.

# About the Author

Charlie Dykstra has been a pulpit minister and Christian counselor for over twenty years. During that time he also did Christian talk radio for eight years and mixed martial arts talk radio for four years. Often, Charlie faced heavy criticism for his activity in mix martial arts from his religious peers. However, he was able to reach out to many young athletes and MMA fans, who otherwise would likely never had shown interest in Christianity.

Charlie is dyslexic and was a poor student in school, for this reason, never pursued his lifelong interest in writing. During his years as a minister, the extent of Charlie\'s creativity was designing religious study materials and some ghostwriting. In time computer programs were developed making a dyslexic author a possibility.

After defeating financial difficulties, with the help of Dave Ramsey\'s Total Money Make Over. He decided it was time to enjoy his freedom and pursue his passion for writing. While working on his first Christian based self-help book, he used the example of pro fighter and friend Johnathan Ivey to illustrate sacrificing for others out of love. The point sprung into a biography.

Charlie is known to lead a busy life. Along with religious commitments, he made room for many things. Charlie has experienced as a competitive freestyle grappler, mixed martial arts coach, color commentator, judge, referee, timekeeper, matchmaker, promoter, and recently became a Representative for ISKA (International Sports Karate/Kickboxing Asociation).

CPSIA information can be obtained
at www.ICGtesting.com
Printed in the USA
LVOW10*0825160518
577327LV00001B/2/P

9 781642 584363